The Ordeal of Mr. Pepys's Clerk

John Harold Wilson

The Ordeal
of Mr. Pepys's Clerk

Ohio State University Press

To Richard D. Altick and Albert J. Kuhn,
maximas gratias

Contents

Preface *ix*

Chapter *One* Enter the Villain *3*

Two Interlude for Plots *17*

Three Winchester House *31*

Four Captain Bedloe *45*

Five Sam Atkins's Dilemma *63*

Six The Terror *79*

Seven The Trial *95*

Eight Tribulation to Triumph *111*

Appendixes *127*

Index *147*

Preface

The strange story of Samuel Atkins, Mr. Pepys's clerk (Mr. Pepys would have said "clark") is true. Even the dialogue is taken verbatim from Atkins's own recollections of his experience and from the stenographic records of his trial. I am responsible for the ordering of events, for the necessary background material, and for descriptions of moods and emotions. In the last I have been guided by a strict concern for Sam Atkins's character as he revealed it in a few personal letters and in his manuscript reports: "An Account of the Passages at my Several Examinations before the Committees of Lords and Commons" and "A Short Narrative of Samuel Atkins, his Case."

The author wishes to express his gratitude to the Bodleian Library, Oxford University, for permission to reproduce manuscript materials from its Department of Western Manuscripts.

J. H. W.

September, 1971

On July 23, 1676, His Majesty's Ketch *Quaker* lay hove-
to in the sun-drenched Mediterranean off the southern
coast of Spain, east of Velèz Malaga. A cable's length
away, the *Quaker*'s convoy, the two hundred ton Dutch
merchantman, *John and Peter*, rolled stolidly in the swell,
a fat sheep guarded by a shepherd dog half her size. A
long gunshot to the east, two Algerine galleys with their
sails furled were rowing slowly toward the little English
warship and its convoy. Beyond them and around the vast
horizon the sea was empty.

A light breeze fluttered the *Quaker*'s sails; without a
strong wind escape was impossible. In a battle the odds
would be formidable. The *Quaker* mounted ten guns, the
John and Peter twelve. One of the Algerines had twenty-
four guns, the other sixteen, and both galleys were crowded
with fighting men, a hundred or more in each. Captain
Charles Atkins had a crew of forty in the *Quaker,* and
Captain Dixworth had no more in the *John and Peter*.
Nevertheless, both ships had their guns loaded and run
out, with gun crews standing by, slow matches smoldering.

Captain Charles Atkins, a tall, military figure in plumed
hat, tucked-up periwig, buff jerkin, and red breeches, stood
on the after deck of the *Quaker*, listening to the arguments
of his warrant officers. Captain Atkins was sweltering in
the heat; he longed for a bottle of Canary in the shade of
his cabin, but he had to make a decision. It was nearly an
hour since the *Quaker* and its convoy had met the corsairs
who barred the way. The Algerines, piratical scourges of

the Mediterranean, had sent a boat to the *Quaker* to learn what ship it had in company and to demand Captain Atkins's pass. By the Anglo-Algerine treaty of 1671, English merchant ships had to carry Admiralty passes in the Mediterranean; English ships of war did not.

Captain Atkins's lofty reply, "This is his Majesty's ketch *Quaker*. My pass is in the muzzles of my guns, and all the ship's company are resolved to die every man rather than go to Algiers," had failed to impress the corsairs, who refused to believe that so small a vessel could be a ship of war. No wonder. The *Quaker* was only fifty-four feet long and eighty tons burden, one of the smallest ships in the English Navy. A hot argument had ended with an ultimatum shouted by a renegade Englishman in the corsair's boat, "Surrender, or we'll sink you!" Now the two galleys were closing in for the kill, ram bows pointed ominously, long oars flashing in the sun.

A brave captain, or at least one with a clean conscience, would have had no reason to hesitate. The Algerines were notoriously poor gunners. A bold front and a couple of volleys from the *Quaker*'s guns might have convinced them of their mistake. If it came to a full engagement, the *Quaker* and the Dutch merchantman might be lucky enough to cripple or sink the frail galleys. At the worst there was honorable death, a sailor's grave, and the satisfaction of knowing that Sir John Narbrough and the Mediterranean Fleet would exact ample revenge. Surrender meant almost certainly the slave markets of Algiers.

But Captain Charles Atkins was neither brave nor honest. At Cadiz, for a fat fee and in defiance of Admiralty orders against "plate carriage," he had taken on board forty thousand dollars in silver and gold for transport to Marseilles, plus fourteen French passengers, whose passage money had gone into his own pockets. In addition he had agreed, for a price, to convoy the Dutch merchantman, now sailing under the English flag, in spite of the fact that the Netherlands were formally at war with Algiers. If he fought, he risked the loss of all his profits, and Captain

Atkins valued profit far above duty and honor. Surely it would be better to take his chances at Algiers, where the English consul, Mr. Samuel Martin, would look after his interests. Captain Atkins, a "gentleman-captain" of aristocratic family, owed his rank to Court favor. He had never sailed before the mast; he had no seamanship; and in his four undistinguished years as a naval officer he had never been in battle.

The *Quaker*'s warrant officers wanted to fight. Jethry Bowman, the sailing-master, John Clange, the boatswain, Edward Alloway, the gunner, Robert Francis, the carpenter, Thomas Wilton, the cook, and Giles Naylor, midshipman, all derided the brown-skinned barbarians in their turbans and flapping gowns. One Englishman, they argued, was worth at least a dozen Turks. Some of the *Quaker*'s crew might die, but even death was better than the stripes, toil, and slow starvation of slaves chained to the oars of Algerine galleys, or the bread-and-water diet, hard labor, and bastinadoes of Moorish farmers. Captain Atkins chewed at his pipe stem nervously. The corsairs, at short range, were turning, bringing their broadsides to bear. Their red gunports opened, showing black muzzles.

Abruptly the captain made his decision, gave an order, and the English Jack fluttered down from the masthead, to a chorus of triumphant yells from the corsairs. The English officers were dumbfounded. Smoothly Captain Atkins explained, "I think it would be a very bad action of me to break the peace at this juncture of time, when so many merchant ships are abroad without convoy. It is better to go to Algiers and dispute it there with the government and the English consul." As the nearest corsair sent a boat with a towing hawser, Captain Atkins found it difficult to meet his officers' eyes.

Fifteen days later, when the galleys towed their prizes into the Bay of Algiers, Consul Samuel Martin learned what had happened and bestirred himself vigorously. His salary was only £100 a year, but there were fees and many chances for lucrative trade on the side. He would not like to lose his post, and he knew that he would be judged in England by the measure of his success in such a crisis. Immediately he made strong representations to the Dey and the general Duana, but in diplomatic terms, careful not to arouse the savagery latent in barbarian breasts. His predecessor, Consul John Ward, had lost his temper and pistolled a Jew in the Dey's presence. The palace guards had promptly cut him to pieces.

Mr. Martin protested as strongly as he dared, even hinting at war, and managed to get the release of the two captive ships and their crews—but not the bullion (which the Algerines insisted was Dutch money) or the fourteen French passengers, who were sold as slaves. On his own authority, Consul Martin removed Captain Atkins from his command and sent him to Tangier, England's military outpost at the entrance to the Straits of Gibraltar. From the officers and crew of the *Quaker* he got the whole story, which he wrote out in detail in a long letter to Mr. Pepys, including with his packet the sworn depositions of the *Quaker's* warrant officers.

At Derby House, Westminster, Samuel Atkins, an Admiralty clerk in the last year of his apprenticeship (no relation to Captain Charles Atkins), opened a packet of letters from Consul Martin at Algiers. The packet looked harmless enough. Sam had no premonition of evil, no sixth sense to tell him that it dealt with the first of a series of events that was to place him in the shadow of the gallows. Reading the contents of the packet was merely a duty, a job to be done. To save his master, Secretary Pepys, from the eyestrain that had forced him to close his shorthand diary seven years ago, Sam Atkins read all incoming letters, winnowing the weighty from the trivial.

It was a sunny afternoon in the autumn of 1676, and the breeze through the open windows facing on the Thames was heavy with the scent of wood smoke and burning leaves. Sam's mind was not on his work; he longed to be out and away. He was wondering how to ask Mr. Pepys's permission to meet some jolly blades for a bite of supper and a merry evening at the Blue Posts in the Haymarket. If he could get away early, he would have time also for a short ramble through Whitehall and St. James's Park, where the beauties of the Town would be on display.

Derby House was in Channel Row, on the bank of the Thames. It was just a step from Derby House to Whitehall, a rambling brick-and-stone palace on the riverbank, where King Charles II lived in regal splendor with his ministers of state and a buzzing swarm of servants. One of his mistresses, the Duchess of Portsmouth, had apartments in the palace; the others had houses nearby. Buck-toothed, childless Queen Catherine lived in Somerset House in the Strand, farther down the river. Now and then the good King paid her a visit.

Whitehall was the center of the Court—a frothy mixture of officeholders, great lords and ladies, country gentlemen, bishops, lawyers, army and navy officers, gamblers, painted courtesans, pickpockets, and politicians. Fashionable London flocked to Whitehall daily to watch the King eat his solitary dinner in the Banqueting Hall, to stroll and gossip in the great stone Gallery, or to idle in St. James's Park beside the canal with its waterfowl or on the banks of Rosamund's Pond. At nineteen, Sam Atkins was still young enough to enjoy the show: the scarlet tunics and bright halberds of the guards, the silver and gold lace of periwigged cavaliers, and the bright satin gowns of bare-shouldered ladies with their hair done in curls and ringlets. Like his master, Sam Atkins loved ease and liberty and had an eye for beauty.

At Derby House everybody worked. Mr. Pepys had his offices and lodgings there, and, as an indentured apprentice, Sam Atkins lived there with his master. Mr. Pepys's regular household consisted of a housekeeper, a butler, a cook, a couple of maids, a footman, and a coachman. Caesare Morelli, a young Fleming and an excellent linguist and musician, was a recent addition to the household. Because he was a Roman Catholic he was looked upon with suspicion by paranoid Protestants.

The Secretary's mistress, Mary Skinner, a young woman of wit and wisdom, was much about the house and helped with the housekeeping and entertaining, but she had private lodgings nearby. She was the daughter of a broken-down merchant, Daniel Skinner, of Mark Lane. Mr. Pepys had begun his affair with her in 1670, a year after the death of his beautiful but trying wife, Elizabeth. Everybody knew about Mary's function and accepted it without question, even her own family and Mr. Pepys's strait-laced friend John Evelyn, who once described Mary as Mr. Pepys's "inclination," and again, in a forgetful moment, as "Mrs. Pepys." It was all very well for the great Mr. Pepys, Secretary to the Office of the Lord High Admiral of England, to keep a mistress openly, but his clerks dared not follow his example. They risked his displeasure by the slightest slip from virtue.

Derby House had private studies for Mr. Pepys and his chief clerk, Will Hewer. Above stairs were "the Lords' room," where the Lords Commissioners of the Admiralty usually met, two or three small offices, and "the great room," where Mr. Pepys's clerks—Atkins, Lawrence, Lewis, Roberts, and Walbanke—usually labored, casting up accounts, checking and filing reports, filling out forms, reading letters, writing letters, and copying letters into "the day book." The large windows of "the great room" overlooked the Thames, the highroad of London, with its bustling traffic of scullers and wherries, the gilded boats of Court officials, barges bringing fruit and vegetables to market, and sloops and hoys loaded with wheat, beef, lumber, and "sea-coal" from Newcastle. The colorful scene was distracting to a bored young clerk with itching feet.

Reluctantly Sam Atkins began to read Mr. Martin's letter. Almost at once he realized that it was truly important; the consul reported an event so horrendous as to be almost beyond belief, an incident that could easily lead to war in the Mediterranean. Hastily Sam skimmed through the letter, glanced at the enclosed depositions, and then hurried to Mr. Pepys's study. There he handed his master the packet with a curt "From Consul Martin, sir."

Little Mr. Pepys, autocrat of England's far ranging navy, sighed wearily, wondering what that fellow Martin had to whine about this time. He was a good consul, but his letters were always prolix and plaintive. Formerly a ship's purser, Mr. Martin owed his appointment as consul to Mr. Pepys—or rather to his own wife (once Betty Lane, one of Mr. Pepys's former mistresses). To salve his conscience, Mr. Pepys always provided well for his cuckolds. He had provided well for himself, too, as his richly furnished study testified: his tapestried chairs, his polished desk and silver standish with pens and ink, and his bookcases with rows of books bound in gleaming calf and stamped with his arms in gold. He was truly in a handsome and thriving condition, with a salary of £ 500 per annum, plus fees.

As he read, Mr. Pepys's face darkened, and under his brown periwig the permanent frown lines in his forehead grew deeper. Sam Atkins, a fair young man with a pleasant face, stood by, awaiting orders. To judge by Mr. Pepys's growing anger this was no time to ask for leave. Briefly he thought about slipping away without permission; perhaps he would not be missed.

Consul Martin's letter concluded:

I hope Captain Atkins and all the English will do me the justice to acquaint your honor that nothing hath been wanting in the performance of my duty, to the hazard of my life and ruin of my family, and without vanity I may tell your honor that if my life would have ransomed this disgrace I had not been now to tell you so. . . . I expect to be made a sacrifice among these people, which I shall embrace with all

humility and content so I die but as I have always
desired to live,

> One of your Honor's most obliged and
> Obedient faithful servants,
> Sa: Martin.

Ordinarily Mr. Pepys dictated his letters, but now his
wrath demanded more direct expression. Selecting a fresh
sheet of paper and dipping his pen, he wrote a short,
vitriolic letter to Captain Charles Atkins at Tangier, ordering him to come home at once to face a court-martial,
and informing him that his cowardly action had resulted
in "such an affront done to his Majesty's flag as cannot,
I think, be remembered to have ever been offered to,
much less borne by, any other." Shameful!

Certainly the Secretary's wrath was justified. An English
warship had tamely surrendered without firing a shot,
and had submitted to a tow, as if it were a helpless hulk!
Shameful, indeed! Unless there were extenuating circumstances, a court-martial would surely sentence Captain
Atkins to death by a firing squad.

But weeks went by without a word from Captain Atkins, who, of course, considered himself innocent and
injured. The Secretary's arm was long, but Tangier was
far away, and gentleman-captains had a convenient habit
of disobeying orders when they chose, sure that easy
King Charles would forgive them. Captain Atkins, a libertine much given to wine and women, was in no hurry
to return to England. Tangier was a garrison town noted
for drunkenness, fornication, gaming, and gluttony, where
more soldiers were killed by the pox and brandy than by
the besieging Moors. It was much more to the captain's
taste than London and a court-martial which might order
him shot. By one excuse or another he managed to delay
his return for months, meanwhile catching a virulent case
of the pox in a Tangier brothel.

At last, too sick to think of more excuses, Captain Atkins returned to England aboard the *Yarmouth,* arriving in February, 1677—eight months after the date of his crime. Of course he could not face his accusers when he was "greatly indisposed by sickness." Generously Mr. Pepys turned him over to the tender care of a chirurgeon and the captain's wife, a lady with a bold and roving eye. Four months later, when the captain had several times been seen walking the streets of London, obviously in good health, the Admiralty Lords asked Mr. Pepys to prepare a court-martial.

Unfortunately, although the Secretary had plenty of affidavits, the crew of the *Quaker* would have to appear in person, and the ketch had recently sailed for the West Indies. A court-martial was impossible; nonetheless Mr. Pepys had the captain arrested and committed to the custody of William Joynes, Gentleman Marshall of the High Court of Admiralty. Captain Atkins promptly appealed to King Charles, asking to be admitted to bail. Most of his relations were alienated by his cowardly conduct, and his father, Sir Jonathan Atkins, Governor of Barbadoes, disowned him; however, various friends and his mother's family, the influential Howards of Cumberland, pleaded for him. Even Mr. Pepys and Sam Atkins strained the quality of mercy in his favor. On July 21, 1677, Captain Charles Atkins was admitted to bail.

Thereafter Captain Charles (still "captain" by courtesy) became a frequent visitor at Derby House—but not to see Mr. Pepys. For the secretary he had only deep and bitter hatred. He held Mr. Pepys responsible for his present plight—discharged, disgraced, indigent, and in danger of shameful death. Behind Mr. Pepys was the authority of the Admiralty Commission and the King himself, but everyone knew that Mr. Pepys (the son of a tailor!) was the real head of the Navy and made all decisions.

This was the second time that Mr. Pepys had injured Charles Atkins. In 1675 the captain of the war ship *Phoenix* died at sea on his way to Barbadoes. When the ship arrived at Bridgetown, Governor Atkins, ignoring the claims of the ship's first lieutenant, appointed his own son, Charles, to command the *Phoenix*. (At the time Charles was only second lieutenant of the *Resolution.*) Charles Atkins brought the *Phoenix* back to England (with two tons of white sugar as his own commercial venture), fully expecting his irregular promotion and command to be confirmed. But Mr. Pepys refused, in spite (he wrote) of his "special regard to my noble friend, your father," and quite properly gave the command to John Howe, first lieutenant of the *Phoenix*. "Right is right," said Mr. Pepys, and then, relenting, gave Charles a captain's pay from the time of the ship's arrival in English waters to the moment when Lieutenant Howe took command—a mere trifle to Charles Atkins. Charles nursed his grudges and bided his time. His gentlemanly gorge rose whenever he thought of Mr. Pepys, an upstart and a mercenary scoundrel!

However, since Captain Charles was not welcome at Court, Derby House was a convenient place in which to while away the time. Hundreds of people came there daily, usually by water to nearby Westminster Stairs. There were seamen seeking warrants or begging for their long overdue pay; officers bringing reports and asking for orders; captains and pursers with long lists of their needs; and merchants wanting news or taking out passes to protect their ships from North African corsairs—twenty-five shillings to Mr. Pepys and ten to his clerks. In the endless stream Captain Charles was always likely to find an old acquaintance from whom he could cadge five or ten shillings—as a temporary loan, of course. If not, at least he could lounge and smoke his pipe in the sheltered garden in summer or by the fire in the "great room" in winter, chat with the clerks, and ask for news of the *Quaker,* now stationed at the Leeward Islands in the West Indies.

He found an easy mark in Sam Atkins, whom the captain called "cousin" because of their common surname.

To the guileless clerk, now barely out of his apprenticeship, the older man was very attractive with his swaggering ways, his pipe in his mouth, and a long sword clanking at his side. Captain Charles was an expert on the customs of brothels and the wiles of whores. He had the easy, supple manners of a courtier, and he could speak casually of his maternal uncles: Charles Howard, Earl of Carlisle; Sir Philip Howard, a justice of the peace and a member of Parliament; and "Northern Tom" Howard, who had married the Dowager Duchess of Richmond. He could describe Court balls and plays and talk about the madcap doings of the King's cockney mistress, Nell Gwyn, the extravagance of his French mistress, Louise, Duchess of Portsmouth, and the escapades of the Queen's maids of honor. Under his spell, Sam Atkins found it difficult to remember the captain's cowardice. He even lent him money, a few shillings at a time.

Sam Atkins's father (also Samuel), a London merchant and "a Presbyterian or Independent zealot," had lived in Scotland for some years, and had been a colonel in the army of Parliament during the Civil War. He returned to London when his son (born August 29, 1657) was two years old, and settled in Limehouse, then a village on the Thames south of London. Sam's mother died when he was very young. Mr. Atkins sent his son to a good school, Bishopshall, in the nearby village of Hackney, where Sam learned his letters, Latin, and "the mathematiques" under Mr. Thomas Walton, a feckless dissenting minister.

Sam was a schoolboy, untouched by disaster, during the second Dutch War, the Great Plague of 1665, and the Great Fire of London in 1666. In 1670 Mr. Atkins died, leaving Samuel and his sister Susannah orphans and well-nigh penniless. Susannah was fifteen years older than Sam. The registers of St. Michael Bassishaw (in the City) record on October 11, 1642, the baptism of Susannah, daughter of Samuel Atkins, merchant, and his wife Hannah.

At thirteen Sam Atkins was apprenticed to Colonel Thomas Middleton, a sturdy old Presbyterian and Surveyor of the Navy, to be bred as a clerk. A year later, when Middleton died, the boy was apprenticed to Mr. Edward Homewood, Clerk of the Survey of the King's Yards at Chatham. In 1674, at the end of the third Dutch War, Mr. Homewood turned him over to Mr. Pepys's chief clerk, Will Hewer, for the remaining three years of his time, which expired in August, 1677.

Sam Atkins was a normal, intelligent, well-trained clerk, like thousands of others to be found in the government offices and counting houses of London. Even his appearance was undistinguished. He was average in height and build, smooth faced, and, because he could not afford a fashionable periwig, with his hair cut short below his ears. Although he was now twenty years old, a full-fledged, responsible clerk living in private lodgings near Derby House, Mr. Pepys still treated him as if he were an apprentice. He kept a severe eye on Sam and made him account for all his time. He was on call by day and by night.

Sam liked his work and did it well. It was exciting to be at the center of affairs, to know that the letter he was writing for Mr. Pepys's signature could send a tall ship to the ends of the earth or move a fleet into battle. Sam could dream of walking the deck of a frigate in the West Indies under sunny skies with green islands abeam, or along the brown Spanish coast in the Mediterranean in search of Barbary pirates.

Of course Sam had the usual assurance of youth, with a tendency to bombast and fustian in speaking and writing. But he was honest, industrious, and pious. Brought up as a zealous Protestant, he went to church often, usually to Whitehall Chapel, where there was very good music, but occasionally to St. Margaret's Church or Westminster Abbey. Sometimes, like his master, he slept through the sermon.

Sam's parents had been strict Puritans. Since the time

of Queen Elizabeth, English Protestants had harried and persecuted those who still clung to the Church of Rome. Of all Protestants, the Puritans were the most fanatical in their hatred of the grim wolf with privy paw, and Sam Atkins shared his parents' bigotry. Once, when a young man of his acquaintance took leave of him in the street, saying that he was going to attend Mass in the Chapel of St. James's Palace (where the King's younger brother, the Catholic Duke of York, held his Court), Sam Atkins said, "Farewell. Go and damn your soul." Sam honestly believed that attendance at a Catholic service was a step on the road to damnation.

In one respect Sam's Puritan conditioning had worn thin. He was inclined to kick over the traces, to be absent from his duties at night without leave, or in the daytime when Mr. Pepys was out of town. At such times he could usually be found with other merry grigs in a nearby tavern, at a playhouse, or at the New Exchange, an arcade in the Strand with booths where comely damsels with smocks cut enticingly low offered for sale linens, gloves, laces, stockings, ribbons, sword-knots, and their own delectable persons. In his best clothes with a sword at his side, Sam Atkins passed for a gentleman.

Once or twice, while he was still an apprentice living in Mr. Pepys's lodgings, Sam had made the mistake of staying out late at night without his master's permission, "for which fault Mr. Pepys did, in April, 1677, express his displeasure against him by turning him away." Friends interceded for Sam, and he wrote a penitent letter, promising his master, "If you please to give me your remission for my past miscarriages and the honor of serving you once more, upon my first ill comportment, or being (on any occasion) found a minute out of your house without your leave, I willingly lay this at your feet as my own act to banish me forever your service, favor, or countenance." Mr. Pepys, who cherished documents, forgave the sinner and kept his letter.

Sam's penitence was real enough; nevertheless, London abounded with delightful taverns where one could drink and be merry with gay companions—chiefly fellow clerks and naval officers. It abounded also with tempting wenches. Sam Atkins was never destined for sainthood, but so far his sins were only venial.

Sam was friendly, generous, considerate, and charitable. Envious Captain Atkins found him an easy touch, despising him even while battening on his bounty. In time, following the well-known principle that one hates the man whom he has wronged, Captain Atkins, a hungry, lean-faced villain, came to hate Mr. Pepys's clerk almost as much as he hated Mr. Pepys.

In the autumn of 1677, partly as a result of Captain Atkins's shameful submission to the Algerine corsairs, England and Algiers were again at war. Few Englishmen knew or cared what the war was about. Algiers was far away, and they had better news to cheer their hearts. King Charles had no legitimate son, and his Catholic brother, James, Duke of York, was heir apparent to the throne. But on October 21, when the King announced the engagement of his niece, Mary, to William of Orange, there was at last hope for a Protestant succession. Over all the land bells rang and bonfires blazed.

The Navy Office had no time for bonfires. In addition to supplying the Mediterranean Fleet, Mr. Pepys had a great project in hand: the building of thirty new ships. The traffic on the Thames and the bustle at Derby House increased. From beleaguered Consul Martin at Algiers came a letter to Secretary Pepys complaining that he had received only £200 for his five years of service and was £1,500 in debt, "for which I must perish here in chains if his Majesty's gracious bounty and your lordship's pity in recommending the same relieve me not." Mr. Pepys had pity enough, but his Majesty's purse was chronically empty.

The seasons changed. The fogs and frosts of winter gave way to the chill rains of spring and the gray skies of a cold English summer. At Algiers, Consul Martin was under house arrest because of popular fury against

England. Later he was moved to a prison, perhaps to protect him from mob violence, He died in prison some time in the late summer of 1678.

That summer Secretary Pepys and his clerks were working still harder, getting a battle fleet ready against the possibility of a war with France. But Sam Atkins still found time for pleasure. Whenever he could take an hour or so off, he was likely to be found at the New Exchange in the Strand. He had two pretty sisters, Anne and Sarah Williams, in chase, and they had a booth in the arcade with finery for sale.

The *Quaker* was still in the West Indies, and Captain Atkins still tramped the London streets, drank in low taverns, or lounged in the great room at Derby House. He nursed his grudges, turned over all sorts of plans in his twisted mind, and borrowed small sums from his friends, including his "cousin," Sam Atkins.

Typical of his petty schemes was one he proposed to Sam in mid-August, 1678. Accompanied by a crony, Captain Henry Hurst, an officer in the Duke of Monmouth's Guards, Captain Charles hunted out Sam in Derby House, found him at work in the Lords room, and told him that Captain Hurst had an acquaintance, a seaman named John Child, who hankered to become a purser and was willing to give Hurst and Captain Charles ten guineas for help in getting an appointment.

"Now," said Captain Charles eagerly, "let's bring the man to you, and do you promise him to do what you can for him, so Captain Hurst and I shall have the ten guineas. You know five guineas will do well this Bartholomew Fair time for me." Bartholomew Fair in West Smithfield was the event of the year for Londoners. For a fortnight there were puppet shows, vulgar drolls, mountebanks, rope dancers, including girls in tights, tumblers, jugglers, freaks, animal acts, strolling whores, and at every turn a booth selling food and drink. Sam wished the captain well, but his request was a nuisance.

"What is the man?" Sam asked. "Has he been at sea? Does he have good certificates?"

"I don't know, faith," said Captain Charles. "We'll bring him to you, and you shall speak with him."

"Well—do," said Sam reluctantly. "But all I can do will signify nothing for him. I can only lay his papers before the Secretary, who, if he appears a good man, will lay them with others before the King when occasion shall offer."

"That's enough," said Captain Charles. Once he had brought the seaman and the clerk together he could claim the guineas. What happened after that was none of his concern.

It was more than enough for Sam's conscience and training. Mr. Pepys, who in his younger days as Clerk of the Acts of the Navy had gloated over gold given him by favored merchants, had grown rich and honest. Now he trained his clerks to beware not only of bribery but even of the appearance of favoritism. Troubled, Sam called Captain Charles to a window out of earshot.

"Pray," he whispered, "don't engage me in this matter to get the poor man's money. I would not do it for never so much."

"No, no," said Captain Charles, "you shall speak with him first." Then, raising his voice, he called, "Captain Hurst, you shall come and dine with me at my lodgings tomorrow and have the man there." Turning to Sam, he added, "And you shall come and dine with us."

"Well—I will. Where do you lodge?"

"I have told you often enough," said Captain Charles, "but you would never be so kind as to come and see me. I lodge near Wild House, just off Drury Lane."

Sam promised to come, and the two captains took their leave, well satisfied. But at noon the next day Sam pretended a press of business and failed to keep the appointment. Much to his relief he heard no more about the matter.

In September, 1678, Sam forgot Captain Charles Atkins's sordid little schemes in the excitement of the Popish Plot, a fantasy dreamed up by a mad Anglican clergyman, Dr. Israel Tonge, and brought to diabolical reality by another clergyman, Titus Oates, the greatest liar in history. He was also a confidence man, a blackmailer, a thief, and a pederast.

Oates was a squat, bandy-legged man with a harsh, nasal voice, a broad, red face, and a chin so long that his mouth seemed to be precisely in the middle of his face. He was nearly thirty. He had been expelled from school; sent down from Cambridge University; charged with perjury; put out of his vicarage at Bobbing, in Kent, for drunkenness and theft; dismissed from a post as naval chaplain for sodomy; and kicked out of a Catholic seminary in Spain and a Catholic college in France.

In London, pretending to be a Catholic, Oates had become acquainted with a number of disguised Jesuits whose mere presence in England made them liable to execution. Some of them had relieved Oates with food and money in his necessity, but Oates had no room for gratitude in his brutish mind. He was motivated by greed, malice, and naked lust for power, partly covered by the loin-cloth of sanctimony.

After several attempts to get attention from skeptical authorities, Oates appeared at last before the Privy Council on September 28 and gave a long, remarkably detailed account of a hellish Jesuit conspiracy to murder King Charles, replace him with his brother and heir-presumptive, the Catholic Duke of York, and bring England back to the Church of Rome by fire and sword. York, too, was to be murdered if he failed to live up to the Jesuits' expectations. Two lay Catholics, Pickering and Grove (said Oates), had already twice tried to assassinate the King, once in January, 1678, and again in March; and Father Coniers, a Jesuit, planned to stab him with a consecrated weapon, a knife with a foot-long blade. There were twenty thousand Catholics ready to rise in arms the moment the King was dead. The Jesuits had appointed five Catholic lords to head the insurrection, and a French army was poised to invade Ireland. Oates gave the names of a hundred priests and lay brothers involved in the conspiracy, plus some two dozen Catholic noblemen and gentlemen.

Oates's account was so circumstantial, and he named names with such assurance, that only the most skeptical could doubt him. At his request, the Council gave him warrants and sent him with a file of musketeers to arrest those he had accused and seize their papers. For the next two days and nights, in pouring rain, Oates was busy routing out and carrying to Newgate Prison dozens of concealed priests and known Catholic laymen, including the Duchess of York's secretary, Edward Coleman. Cynical King Charles, rightly convinced that Oates was a liar, refused to take him seriously and went off to the autumn horse races at Newmarket. There, on October 11, fortunate Mr. Pepys joined him for a long weekend.

Had it not been for sheer luck, Oate's fragile structure of lies might have collapsed under its own weight. However, among Coleman's confiscated letters were some with phrases that could easily be construed as referring to a Popish Plot. English Protestants speculated and stirred uneasily. They all knew about the fires of Smithfield in the reign of Bloody Queen Mary and the Gunpowder Plot of 1605, celebrated with fireworks and "pope-burnings" every November 5, Guy Fawkes Day. They remembered the massacres by Irish Catholics in 1641 and the Great Fire of London, presumably set by Catholics. Moreover, they were constantly aware of the menace from Catholic France, whose king, Louis XIV, believed himself to be divinely appointed to drive heresy from all Europe, and whose armies now threatened Protestant Holland.

In October speculation turned to certainty. On Saturday, October 12, a date to remember, Sir Edmund Bury Godfrey, a melancholy, conscientious justice of the peace, left his London home and was seen no more alive. Five days later two rustics stumbled on his body in a ditch at the foot of Primrose Hill, north of London. He had been beaten and strangled, his neck had been broken, and his own sword had been thrust through his heart after death. He had not been robbed.

Now it so happened that three weeks before Oates revealed his Plot to the Privy Council, he had taken a written "Narrative" to Justice Godfrey and had sworn to the truth of his statements. When this fact became known, the truth was clear as daylight to a suspicious and frightened nation—Godfrey had been murdered by Papists because he knew too much. Nations, like men, are subject to spasms of mindless hate, during which they will believe anything, no matter how incredible.

Strangely enough, omniscient Titus Oates did not know who had killed Justice Godfrey; at least he accused no one. To this day no one knows who murdered the magistrate—perhaps mad Philip Herbert, Earl of Pembroke, who owed Godfrey a grudge. No matter. Every English Protestant knew beyond the shadow of a doubt that the Jesuits, fiends from hell, were guilty. Oates had told the truth about the Plot; suddenly he was "the Savior of the Nation."

Uneasiness boiled up to an orgy of mass hysteria as rumors multiplied. The body of Sir Edmund Bury Godfrey (said a contemporary, Roger North) "was brought to town with a prodigious attendance of rabble and laid in the street exposed to the view of all comers, and all that saw it went away inflamed." Cannon surrounded Whitehall Palace, and men searched the cellars under the Parliament House for concealed gunpowder. The trained bands of London patrolled the streets day and night; every Protestant went armed with sword and pistol, and ladies carried pistols in their muffs. Sir Thomas Player, a London alderman, voiced the common fear in deathless words, "I do not know but the next morning we may all rise with our throats cut."

On October 19, King Charles issued a proclamation offering a reward of £500 to anyone who could discover Godfrey's murderers, plus a pardon if the discoverer was an accomplice. It was all the government could do. The police force of London consisted of citizen watchmen for each ward—decrepit Dogberrys who tippled in taverns instead of patrolling the streets—incompetent parish constables, the City trained bands, the sheriffs' posses, and the King's Guards. There were no detectives, no investigators except for a few energetic justices of the peace who issued warrants, searched for and captured culprits, examined them, committed them to prison, and gave evidence at their trials. The law courts had their bailiffs and the Secretaries of State their King's Messengers to serve warrants on information received. "Thief-takers," who made a trade of recovering stolen goods and were usually in league with the thieves, did a thriving business. Informers, "knights of the post," who profited from offered rewards, were mercenaries willing to swear to anything for a fee. Now, craving the offered reward of £500, dozens of informers crawled out of their holes to pester the Secretaries with "informations."

On October 21, Parliament met, and the Popish Plot took on a new dimension. The party long in opposition to King and Court, called variously "the country party," "the faction," "the fanatics," or "the mutineers," and soon to be known as the Whigs, was a loose coalition of republicans, dissenters, tightfisted country gentlemen, monied merchants, opportunists, and malcontents opposed, they said loudly, to "Popery and Arbitrary Power." The party was sometimes led by "the great little lord," Anthony Ashley Cooper, Earl of Shaftesbury. Physically Shaftesbury was a small man, worn with years and a suppurating ulcer in his side kept open by a drain, or tap, but his fiery spirit overrode his weakness. (Among beggars and thieves a gallon pot of wine with a tap was called "a Shaftesbury.")

Shaftesbury was a brilliant orator, an able administrator, and a ruthless politician. He had been great in Cromwell's government; with the Restoration he turned cat-in-pan and became great in the government of Charles II. He was successively Chancellor of the Exchequer, a Commissioner of the Treasury, and finally Lord Chancellor. Now he was in opposition; his enemies called him "Lord Shiftsbury."

Between Shaftesbury and James, Duke of York, an obstinate and vindictive bigot, there was war to the knife. Shaftesbury knew that he was doomed if the Catholic Duke ever succeeded to the throne. Motivated partly by self-interest and lust for power, and partly by honest fear of a Catholic king, Shaftesbury bent all his energies to his major project: excluding York from the succession to the throne—by any necessary means. Expediency is the last refuge of patriots.

Shaftesbury did not invent the Popish Plot, but he was quick to see its usefulness to his cause. When Parliament convened, it promptly sent to the Tower the five lords accused by Oates as leaders of the Catholic insurrection. Each House appointed a committee to investigate Godfrey's murder and the Plot in general. Shaftesbury and a few of his cronies on the Lords' committee formed a Secret Committee within the larger body to examine prisoners, question witnesses and informers, and read confiscated papers, looking for anything that might tend to incriminate Catholics, but particularly for evidence pointing to the Duke of York as an accessory to Godfrey's murder.

Meanwhile, the London magistrates enforced the penal laws against Catholics, harried them as recusants, ransacked their houses for arms and seized their best horses. Officeholders, fearing they might be accused as Papists, hastened to take the Anglican Sacrament and the oath against the Doctrine of Transubstantiation as required by the Test Act of 1673. In the universal madness, no man was safe.

Merely to doubt the reality of the Plot left one open to charges of being Popishly affected. Mr. Pepys, who had no love for Papists, had his doubts, but wisely said nothing.

Like all extreme Protestants, Sam Atkins believed whole-heartedly in the Plot. When, at Parliament's request, the King issued a proclamation banning all Catholics at least ten miles from London, Sam was delighted. "By God," he said to his friend, John Walbanke, "I am glad of it, for now we shall be rid of them."

The Opposition Party took over the Plot, pouring oil on the flames of panic. On October 31, six men in long black cloaks carried a coffin with the rotting flesh of Sir Edmund Godfrey through streets lined with roaring mobs, to St. Martin's Church. In solemn procession before the coffin marched seventy-two clergymen in their robes; behind it came more than a thousand gentlemen on foot, all in deep mouring. Dr. William Lloyd, the eloquent rector of St. Martin's, mounted to the pulpit, guarded by two stalwart gentlemen in parson's robes. The burden of his funeral sermon was a violent denunciation of Catholics. "The crowd was prodigious," said Roger North, "both at the procession and in and about the church, and so heated that anything called Papist, were it cat or dog, had probably gone to pieces in a moment."

In all the tumult and shouting, Captain Charles Atkins, ostensibly a Protestant, but a man without faith or conviction, looked, listened, and bided his time. Penniless and deeply in debt, he saw "Doctor" Titus Oates, the great informer, now with lodgings in Whitehall Palace, servants, guards, and a pension of £600 a year. Why shouldn't Captain Charles become an informer and get the £500 reward offered for Godfrey's killers? At least, by coming forward zealously as a King's witness, he could win favor at Court and get the King's ear again. Then all would be plain sailing; he could convince the easy King of his innocence in the *Quaker* affair and get his command again. All he needed was a plausible story to swear to at the cost of a little perjury—in seventeenth-century law no more than a misdemeanor. Of course, godly people believed that one who swore falsely endangered his immortal soul, but Captain Charles was sure that God would never damn a gentleman for a few lies.

He thought of his new acquaintance, John Child, the seaman he had asked Sam Atkins to prefer to a purser's place. (Sam's cavalier treatment of his request still rankled; it had cost the captain five golden guineas.) Child was a proper man for a plot. He was a shady character, a desperate fellow with dubious antecedents and some queer friends, among them one Owens, "a captain in the French sea service"—probably a spy. Since their first meeting in August, Captain Charles and Child had often met and drunk together at a tavern, The Three Tobacco Pipes in Holborn.

Cautiously Captain Charles cooked up his "information," let a whiff of it reach the Secretaries' noses, and on October 30 served it to the Privy Council, piping hot and garnished with his oath. (He had no written "narrative," but Secretary Williamson kept notes.)

Early in October, said the captain, very impressive in his best uniform, he met John Child by chance in Holborn Fields and at his request went with him to a shed at the backside of The Three Tobacco Pipes, where they could be private. After the master of the house had brought each a pot of ale, Child remarked that he knew all about the captain's necessities and troubles and suggested that he might undertake a project that would put money in his purse.

"I replied," said Captain Charles, "anything that was honorable I would undertake, or that became a gentleman, but to rob on the highway, or anything of that nature that was base, I would not do it. He answered me that it was a thing of greater moment than that. He told me it was the killing of a man"—presumably Godfrey, although Captain Charles never mentioned the prospective victim's name.

Virtuously, Captain Charles refused to become a party to murder. Child, he said, gave him eight or nine days to think over the proposition, promising him a great reward if he joined with a group described only as "them." Some days later Captain Charles met Child at another tavern, The Three Cans in Holborn. "He told me," said the captain, "if I would not agree with them to help to murder him, yet if I would conceal it, I should have £100 brought to my chamber; but if I did reveal it, I should not outlive it." At the risk of his life and the loss of £100, courageous Captain Charles was now revealing the plot. Asked if he knew or could say anything more about the affair, Captain Charles replied, "No."

The Privy Council was not impressed. As an informer, Captain Charles was a rank amateur; he lacked the monumental brass of a Titus Oates. Here is vague talk of "him" and "them," but no prominent names, no mention of Catholics and Jesuits, no oaths sealed in blood, no secret midnight meetings, no promises of absolution for murder or of masses to be said for conspirators' souls—nothing, in short, to tie Captain Atkins's little fairy tale to Godfrey's murder or the Popish Plot.

John Child, brought in to confront his accuser, denied everything, asserting that he had been playing cards with Owens and Captain Charles in the shed behind The Three Tobacco Pipes on October 2. The Privy Council threw up its collective hands, thanked Captain Charles, and dismissed him. However, as a precaution, the Council sent Child to Newgate. One never knew.

For two days Captain Charles, aware of his failure, thought things over. He realized his mistake: he had been too cautious, too fearful of committing himself and naming names. Clearly the Council wanted a culprit of more substance and rank than a mere out-of-work sailor. Full of self-pity and brooding over his wrongs, Captain Charles thought of Secretary Pepys, the man responsible for his present plight. Captain Charles could justify anything he did to Mr. Pepys on the ground of simple self-defense. He knew that the *Quaker* would soon be on its way home, and he would have to face a court-martial. (In fact, the *Quaker* did not leave the Leeward Islands until Christmas, 1678.)

Surely Captain Charles could think of some way to involve Mr. Pepys in the Godfrey affair, if only to throw him off-balance and stall off the court-martial! He could hardly accuse Mr. Pepys himself of murder; the Secretary had been at Newmarket at the time of the killing. But he could have hired a desperado—John Child, perhaps. Could Captain Charles make a fresh discovery, involve Sam Atkins in what he had already deposed about Child, and through the clerk involve the master? How could Captain Charles plume up his will in double knavery—and win £500?

On the morning of November 1, Captain Atkins's uncle, Sir Philip Howard, a justice of the peace for Middlesex and Westminster, took his nephew's Examination under oath. Perhaps Sir Philip, a member of the Opposition and a friend of Shaftesbury, coached the deponent in some particulars, but we must be careful not to take the credit away from Captain Charles. His was the material, the prime motive, and the means. Much later, good Mr. Pepys, in a reminiscent mood, commented that "my endeavor to bring Captain Atkins to an account made him play the rogue against me through my Atkins, and so rewarded me also for my mercy to him in getting him bailed."

According to the Examination, "Charles Atkins, Esquire, saith that in Derby House, being in discourse with Samuel Atkins (clerk to Mr. Pepys, Secretary of the Admiralty), the said Samuel did say "That Sir Edmund Bury Godfrey had very much vilified his master, and that if he lived long would be the ruin of him.' Upon which the said Samuel did ask this examinant 'Whether he did think Child to be a man of courage and secresy?' To which this examinant did reply, 'That the said Child had been at sea, and had behaved himself very well, as he had been informed.' Upon which the said Samuel did bid this examinant 'Send the said Child to his master, Mr. Pepys, but not to him, the said Samuel, for that he would not be seen to know anything of it.'

"This examinant did endeavor to find out the said Child, but did not meet with him till the day after (this discourse had happened between him and Samuel Atkins) at The Three Tobacco Pipes in Holborn, where this examinant did tell Child 'That Secretary Pepys would speak with him.' And the next time that this examinant did see the said Child (after that he had given him that direction), he, the said Child, did endeavor to engage the said examinant to join with him in the murder of a man; the particulars of which this examinant hath declared before the King and Council, Wednesday last past."

Captain Charles had learned his lesson well. Now, without directly saying so, he implied that Godfrey was murdered by John Child at Mr. Pepys's instigation. Of course, Samuel Atkins could deny that the reported conversation ever took place, but Captain Charles was sure that the clerk was a weak, soft-headed man, easily frightened and as pliable as wet leather. There was no danger from that quarter.

As in duty bound, Sir Philip Howard filed the Examination with Secretary of State Coventry and then hurried to tell my Lord Shaftesbury about it. As he listened, Shaftesbury's thin lips cracked in a smile. Mr. Pepys of the Navy, eh? Excellent! Lord Shaftesbury had an old bone to pick with that gentleman.

In February, 1674, Mr. Pepys had been denied the seat in the House of Commons to which he had just been elected by the borough of Castle Rising. One of the charges against him was that he was a crypto-Catholic. It was reported that a great man, Lord Shaftesbury himself, had seen an altar and a crucifix in Mr. Pepys's earlier residence in Seething Lane. Pressed by a committee of the House to confirm or deny the report, Shaftesbury had hesitated, quibbled, claimed loss of memory, and finally had refused to testify either way. After some trouble, Mr. Pepys's election was allowed to stand. However, Shaftesbury's ungentlemanly conduct had drawn from Mr. Pepys an angry, indiscreet letter, in effect accusing the earl of malice. Shaftesbury had made no reply, but he had a long memory.

Much more important was the fact that Mr. Pepys, supposedly a good Protestant, had been the Duke of York's favorite when the Duke was Lord High Admiral, before the Test Act had forced York, as a Catholic, to resign his high place. Indeed, Mr. Pepys, though deploring the Duke's Catholicism, was still loyal to his former patron; and York had a great deal of influence in naval affairs, even though the Admiralty was now headed by Lords Commissioners. If Lord Shaftesbury could get at Mr. Pepys, he could strike a shrewd blow at the Duke through him.

Of course, Shaftesbury mused, Captain Atkins is a coward and a rogue in grain, and his story is pretty thin; it may well be a cheat, a gull, and the members of Parliament may refuse to swallow it. Still, if we can't bring them to swallow worse nonsense than this, we shall never do anything with them. The end justifies the means.

Late that afternoon the Lords' Secret Committee sent a message to Secretary Coventry asking him to send to the Marquis of Winchester's house in Lincolns Inn Fields the Examination of Charles Atkins, the depositions made by Charles and John Child before the Privy Council, and "the body of Samuel Atkins."

Night came early on Friday, November 1, but Mr. Thomas Smith, King's Messenger, was in no hurry to serve Secretary Coventry's warrant. Shortly after five o'clock, he accompanied a friend to the Rhenish wine house in Channel Row, sat down at the fireside with a bottle, and by a porter sent word to Derby House that he wished to see Mr. Samuel Atkins. Presuming that he was needed on naval business, Sam told his fellow clerk, John Walbanke, where he was going, and sauntered around to the tavern at his leisure. Mr. Smith told him that Secretary Coventry wanted to see him.

Readily enough, Sam agreed to go to Whitehall, but he wondered what the problem was and why a messenger was sent to fetch him. Mr. Smith, a chuckle-headed fellow, refused to explain, but he showed Sam a warrant for his arrest, saying that he had been ordered not to show it unless Mr. Atkins refused to go with him.

"There's no need for a warrant," said Sam jauntily, "I am free to go with you." He was shocked when Mr. Smith asked for his sword. Uneasily he searched his memory for a rule he had broken or a crime he had committed unwittingly, but his conscience was clear.

At Secretary Coventry's office in Whitehall he waited with Mr. Smith until the Secretary returned from his supper. Then he waited again while Mr. Coventry wrote a letter to Lord Shaftesbury. No one would tell him what he was wanted for. Surely there must be a mistake somewhere.

Mystified and apprehensive, Sam got into a hackney coach with the King's Messenger. The night was bitterly cold. The streets were almost empty and completely dark except for the occasional gleam of a candle-lit window or the flicker of a lantern hanging beside a door. But Sam Atkins knew his city, and in spite of his panic he recognized landmarks—the rumble of the coach wheels on cobbles here and gravel there, the darker loom of a building, or the stink of a lay-stall where night soil was piled to dry.

It was a long drive up King Street and St. Martin's Lane to Longacre Street, and thence through Great Queen Street to Lincolns Inn Fields. The coach turned into the driveway of Winchester House, a big, square, brick-and-stone mansion, standing well back from the street. Its windows, ablaze with candles, were almost dimmed by the flaring torches held by servants in the courtyard, where half a dozen coaches waited. The horses' breath steamed in the frosty air.

Now thoroughly frightened, his heart pounding, Sam Atkins followed Mr. Smith into the great hall, where they stayed while a footman carried Secretary Coventry's letter up the stairs. When the servant came down and beckoned, they followed him up the wide stairs to an upper hall. Mr. Smith pushed Sam through a doorway guarded by soldiers and said goodbye—his mission completed.

Sam found himself in a large, warm, comfortably furnished room, redolent of tobacco, wine, and apple wood burning in the fireplace. Six lords, members of the Secret Committee, elegant gentlemen in silks and satins, with broad-brimmed, feathered hats perched atop their great periwigs, were clustered together at a table, examining some papers by the light of a chandelier. In his black cloak, gray coat and breeches, Sam Atkins looked like a magpie among birds of paradise.

Sam recognized the lords: hawk-faced Lord Shaftesbury, seated at the table, a little man, pale and drawn, with his face half hidden by a fair periwig; the burly Duke of Buckingham, still notorious for his scandalous affair with Lady Shrewsbury, his once handsome visage reddened and bloated by dissipation; Lord Halifax, a dignified gentleman with a lean, intellectual face; Henry Compton, Bishop of London, who, even in his flat hat, silk gown, and cassock, still looked like the soldier he had been before taking orders; the Earl of Essex, a man of uneasy temper, quick to wrath; and the Committee's host, the eccentric Marquis of Winchester, who said very little. Another gentleman, somewhat apart and clearly not a member of the Committee, turned out to be Captain Atkins's uncle, Sir Philip Howard.

It was an imposing display of wealth and power. In spite of his middle-class independence, Sam had learned from Mr. Pepys to respect authority. Quite without thinking, he took off his hat.

Lord Shaftesbury looked up from his papers and crooked a finger at Sam, who stumbled toward the table. My lord assessed the frightened clerk at a glance and smiled. An easy cully, he thought.

"Know you, Mr. Samuel Atkins," said my lord gently, "one Master, or Captain, Atkins?"

Sam found his voice with an effort. "Yes, my lord," he croaked.

"How long have you known him?"

"About two or three years, I think."

"Are you related?"

"No, my lord." Sam hesitated and then volunteered, "Only for names' sake we have called cousin."

Lord Shaftesbury nodded and smiled. His manner was kindly, almost paternal.

"Do you think, or believe, he has any reason to do you a prejudice?"

Sam's memory leaped to the affair of Captain Charles and the seaman who hoped to become a purser, but his judgment quickly rejected it. "No, my lord, I know of none."

"Did you ever tell him, in your discourse about the Plot, that there was no kindness—or a want of friendship, I think 'twas—betwixt Mr. Pepys and Sir Edmund Godfrey?"

Sam was more mystified than ever. What stuff was this? What was it leading to? "No, my lord, I never mentioned Sir Edmund Godfrey's name to him in my whole life upon any occasion that I remember, nor ever talked with him about the Plot."

Lord Essex broke in abruptly. "Do you know one Child?" he barked. Child? Sam hesitated; he vaguely remembered the name of Josiah Child, merchant.

"No, sir. I have heard of such a man's having been concerned in the victualing of the Navy, but to my knowledge I never saw him."

"No, no," said Lord Essex testily. "This is another sort of a man, and one whom you will be found to know very well."

Sam Atkins, who prided himself on his memory, was nettled. He was rapidly regaining his self-confidence. Instead of charging him with a crime, the lords were treating him like a schoolboy, caught out of bounds. "My lord," he replied sharply, "if upon seeing him I shall so, I wont fail to own it."

"Pray, then," Lord Essex said to a footman standing by the door leading to an inner room, "call Child in." In a moment John Child appeared, hat in hand. He was a very ordinary, nondescript fellow, by his garb a seaman.

"Do you now not know this man?" asked Lord Essex.

"No, my lord," Sam replied positively, "I never saw him in my life to my remembrance."

Lord Essex glared at Sam and then turned to Child. "What say you, Child? Know you this person?"

"No, my lord," Child mumbled, twisting his hat in his hands nervously, "I never saw him in my life."

Lord Essex sat back, scowling. Lord Shaftesbury took command again, sent Child away, and called for Captain Charles Atkins, who swaggered in through another door, his ever-present clay pipe in his hand. Sam saluted him, but the captain avoided meeting his "cousin's" eyes.

"Pray, Mr. Charles Atkins," said Lord Shaftesbury, "what did Samuel Atkins tell you of Mr. Pepys and Sir Edmund Godfrey?"

It was a moment of triumph for Captain Charles. Once more he was a personality, a man of importance. Now he could even the score with Sam Atkins, the mere clerk before whom he had abased himself so often to beg for a loan.

"My lord," he said smoothly, "he told me there was a difference 'twixt his master and Sir Edmund Godfrey, and I asked him if Sir Edmund Godfrey were a Parliament man or no, and he said no. I asked him whether the difference was upon the occasion of Mr. Pepys being formerly accused for a Catholic in the House of Commons, and he said no, 'twas upon this occasion—"

Upon this occasion? What occasion? Sam Atkins was puzzled and angry. He had never had such a conversation with Captain Charles, and he knew very well that there had never been a difference between Mr. Pepys and Justice Godfrey.

"My lord," he said, keeping his temper with difficulty, "I know not what has led Captain Atkins to say this. I assure you I never told him in my life one word of it, never talked to him about the Plot, or mentioned Sir Edmund Godfrey's name to him—that I remember—on any occasion. I am sure that I never made him a subject for any discourse."

The lords lifted their eyebrows and looked their disbelief, but Lord Shaftesbury was still genial, almost coaxing, as if Sam Atkins were a child to be wheedled. "Did you not ask Charles Atkins whether this Child was a man of courage and secrecy, and bid Charles Atkins send him to Derby House to enquire for your master, but be sure not to ask for you?"

Sam was outraged. "No, my lord, not in my life one word like it."

"You know, Mr. Atkins," said Captain Charles, carefully staring at his pipe, "this discourse was between us in your large room in the window."

"Captain Atkins," cried Sam, finally losing his temper, "God, your conscience, and I know 'tis notoriously untrue. The last time I saw you at Derby House was on Monday, the twenty-first of October, Mr. John Beverly, lieutenant of the *Mountague,* being there, which I remember because we all three came out of Derby House together about one o'clock and parted in King Street. I went to dinner, and you two went toward Whitehall, Mr. Beverly, to whom I talked all the way going, having invited me to dine the next day at his house, which I did.

"All that passed between us then—our stay together alone being not half a quarter of an hour—was that coming all three out of the little office together you pulled me to the window in the large room and asked me to lend you five shillings, to which I said aye, and so going downstairs I stayed back—Mr. Beverly going down first—and pulled you by the coat and put the crown in your hand to prevent Beverly observing it. This was the last time I saw you. The time before was in August, about the middle, a little before Bartholomew Fair."

Once well under way, with adrenalin flooding his veins, Sam Atkins could not be stopped until he had had his say. He went on to tell the story of Captain Atkins, Captain Hurst, and the seaman who wanted to be a purser. "Possibly you might name his name and it might be Child, but I don't remember it." Sam had avoided going to dinner at Captain Atkins's lodgings, even though at noon, near Wallingford House, he had met the Captain's handsome wife, who told him he was "expected and stayed for at her house," and coaxed him to come. Sam thought he was well rid of a dirty business. "And I did not see Captain Atkins again until the aforesaid twenty-first of October."

There was a moment's silence when Sam had finished. Captain Atkins made no denial, but he moved slowly out of earshot. The Secret Committee refused to comment.

Its members were not interested in the truth. United in their hatred of the Duke of York, they sought a weapon against him. Sam Atkins might be the arrow to fit their bowstring.

"Come, Mr. Atkins," said Lord Shaftesbury quietly, "you are a seeming hopeful young man, and truly, for aught I see, a good ingenuous one. Captain Atkins has sworn this positively against you, to whom he bears no malice, but has acknowledged several obligations. Besides, to tell you truth, I don't think him to have wit enough to invent such a lie. Prithee, be ingenuous with us, and tell us whether you said this or no."

I assure your lordship," Sam protested, "upon my faith, which I am ready to bind with my oath if you please, I never said one word in all my life like it."

"Why," said Shaftesbury, "we believe Mr. Charles Atkins to be a man that has loved wine and women and been a debauched man, but whence would you have us think him a rascal?"

"Why, my lord, this I would offer to you—only submitting it to you—how much a coward is to be judged so." Then Sam told the story of the *Quaker* ketch and Captain Atkins' cowardly submission to the Algerine rovers, an action for which he was still a prisoner on bail. The lords let him talk, two whispering together, one drumming on the table, another turning over papers. Clearly nobody cared what kind of a man Captain Atkins was.

Lord Shaftesbury was beginning to lose his patience; he decided to try a different approach. Perhaps the clerk was popishly affected.

"Pray, Sam Atkins," he said, "what religion are you of?"

"My lord," Sam replied proudly, "a Protestant, and my whole family before me."

"Did you ever receive the Oath and the Sacrament?"

"No, my lord, but I was under an intention to do it on Sunday."

" 'Tis time," sneered Lord Essex.

"Well, now you wont do it, I am sure," said Shaftesbury, with his most winning smile, "You can't forgive Captain Atkins."

"Yes, my lord, I assure you I can and do, and to show you it, I forgive him too the debt he owes me—'twixt forty and fifty shillings—and I am ready to take the Sacrament with a clear conscience. I confess I have not done it, not thinking myself obliged by any employment I had to do it, as being a menial servant; and many thousands of my age— good Protestants—will be found not to have done it also."

"How long have you lived with Mr. Pepys?"

"Four years last August."

"How old are you?"

"Twenty-one years the twenty-ninth of last August."

"Where did you live before you came to Mr. Pepys?"

Sam Atkins had last lived with Mr. Homewood at Chatham, but he knew that Colonel Middleton, his first employer, and Lord Shaftesbury had been friends. He shaded the truth.

"I lived formerly with Colonel Middleton."

"Well," said Shaftesbury, disappointed of his hopes, "I am sure he was a Protestant. But now you are brought up to business and have access to Catholic St. James's, 'tis to be feared you may be otherwise, for we are apt to suspect people inclining to the sea."

"My lord, I assure you I never had temptations from without or within to alter my religion, I thank God, and I hope I never shall."

Now the burly Duke of Buckingham came around the table and loomed over the clerk; his breath was heavy with the fumes of brandy. "Well, Sam Atkins," he said, with a finger on Sam's forehead, "I never saw you before, but I'll swear you're an ingenuous man. I see the working of your brain. Pray, declare what you know of this matter, whether you did say these words or no."

The other lords—all but Shaftesbury—gathered around Sam, urging him in friendly fashion to tell the truth, to confess everything, to admit that Captain Atkins had quoted him correctly, that he had indeed sent word to Child to come and see Mr. Pepys. But the clerk's blood was up. He realized now that the Committee was after Godfrey's killer, and that in some obscure way Captain Atkin's lies pointed to Mr. Pepys as the suborner of murder—a ridiculous notion. Stubbornly Sam declared his inability to say what the Committee wanted him to say. Again and again he declared that Captain Atkins had lied. Sam's conscience was bolstered by love for his master and by fear of what Mr. Pepys might say or do. The mixture was unbeatable.

At last Lord Shaftesbury ordered Sam and Captain Atkins out of the room. Sam had barely time to catch his breath and try to steady his whirling brain before he was called in again. Cajolery had failed; now the Committee would try threats. The lords were ominously silent and gloomy. Lord Shaftesbury wore his grimmest look, a look to strike terror into the hardiest criminal.

"Mr. Atkins," he said, "we are to be plain with you. Here's a positive oath against you." He paused to let the significance of his statement sink in. Sam Atkins knew what he meant. Fundamental in English law was the belief that no Christian would swear falsely; therefore, a positive oath sworn against a prisoner at the bar of justice was taken as proof of his guilt. Juries considered the accused guilty until he could prove his innocence. If the lords did not accept Sam's denials, how could he hope for credit with a jury? How could he prove Captain Atkins a liar?

Watching his victim's face keenly, Shaftesbury continued, "We can't answer to Parliament the doing less than committing you to Newgate."

Newgate! Rebuilt since the Great Fire of 1666, Newgate Prison, a foul and noisome rabbit-warren of cells, common rooms, and underground cellars, was the terror of evil-doers. No doubt the lords could commit Sam; behind them was the crushing power of Parliament. For a moment Sam was dismayed, but his sturdy courage met the challenge.

"What your lordships please," he said. "If you send me to be hanged, I could say no more, or otherwise."

Again the lords pressed him to tell everything he knew. He would not be harmed if he did so—he was not himself involved—he was in no danger unless he concealed information about a crime—there were certain rewards. But their words broke on the solid rock of Sam's integrity.

"My lords," he said, a little pompously perhaps, "the telling a lie will do me a great deal of hurt, and I trust I never shall. But I must tell a lie if I say otherwise than what I have already said."

Sir Philip Howard made a last appeal which was also a threat. "Mr. Atkins, you have not lived so long in an office but you know the laws of the nation to be such as will bring you under severe punishment if you be found to conceal or cloak anything of this nature. You bring yourself in accessory to it by doing so."

True enough; it was a hanging matter. Well, so be it. Sam's early Puritanism had taught him fatalism, to accept martyrdom at the hands of the wicked. "Sir," he replied, "I very well know it, and I know also the laws of God bring me under a worse guilt if I tell a lie, which I must do if I say anything in this matter different from what I have done." There was a higher law that said "A false witness shall not be unpunished, and he that speaketh lies shall perish." Sam Atkins knew his Bible and could always find an apt quotation to bolster and sustain a heroic pose. Beset, harassed, and frightened as he was, such is the contrariety of human nature that he could find joy in defying his accusers, come what might.

Lord Shaftesbury saw that further threats would be useless. Let the foolish young man have time to consider his plight, time for the fear of death to overcome his scruples. It would be best to treat him gently; it would never do to throw him into a dungeon in irons, and torture would merely stiffen his Puritan stubbornness. Besides, Mr.

Pepys, a man to be reckoned with, would make the welkin ring twice if he learned that his favorite clerk was being ill-treated.

Shaftesbury called in Captain William Richardson, the Keeper of Newgate, who waited in the hall with John Child in a warder's custody, gave him instructions and a warrant committing Samuel Atkins to prison for "felony in concealing the murder of Sir Edmund Bury Godfrey," and turned to more important business. The hour was late, but he was thinking of delivering a speech at the next day's session of the House of Lords, demanding that the Duke of York be dismissed from the Privy Council. He wanted to consult with his colleagues.

Sam Atkins stumbled from the room with the Keeper, only half seeing Captain Charles's mocking smile in the hallway. In the frosty courtyard Captain Richardson and Child's warder bundled their charges into a waiting coach. The cold night air was a pleasant shock. Sam could almost feel his mind clearing as the coach lurched down Holborn Hill, across Holborn Bridge, and down Snow Hill to Newgate.

The ill-omened twin towers of the prison, with their sculptures of Justice, Mercy, and Truth, were ghost-like in the glimmer of the jailers' lanterns; the entrance a black, yawning mouth as the gates creaked open. The passageway stank of urine and excrement. Inside, past the lodge where felons were fettered, the air was thick with the stench of decay, mildew, unwashed bodies, vomit, and rotten flesh.

John Child, who had previously paid his entrance fee of eleven shillings and sixpence and his "easement" fee of ten shillings and sixpence to be free of his shackles, disappeared with his warder toward the Felons' Common Side, where there was neither air nor light, coals nor blankets. Sam Atkins was luckier. He was not chained; he was not even required to pay entrance or easement fees. Captain Richardson, a taciturn man, led him past the entrance lodge to the Keeper's quarters, took him upstairs to a spartan chamber with a sea-coal fire, a bed, a stool, and a chamber-pot, and left him with a curt "good night," locking the door after him.

Sam Atkins sat on the stool by a barred window overlooking the street. Suddenly he was exhausted and aware that he had missed his usual supper of bread and cheese. Deprived of his audience of tormentors, he could give himself up to despair. He was alone with his whirling thoughts, the all-pervading prison stench, the far-off screams of rage and laughter from the Felons' Common Side, and the distant, monotonous voice of the bellman, the sexton of St. Sepulchre's Church, in the street before the prison gate.

"You prisoners who are within," he chanted, ringing his handbell, "who for wickedness and sin, after many mercies shown you, are now appointed to die tomorrow morning—" Was Sam Atkins to die? Surely, but not tomorrow; there would have to be a trial first, and Mr. Pepys would help him. But what chance would he have against the Attorney General and the merciless Committee of Lords? Why not go along with the cheat and let Mr. Pepys look to himself? Briefly Sam was tempted—but, no, "Thou shalt not bear false witness against thy neighbor," especially if the neighbor was Mr. Pepys.

"—the great bell of St. Sepulchre shall toll for you in form of and manner of a passing bell as used to be tolled for those who are at the point of death—" Aye, better to die with dignity than face the wrath of God—or of Mr. Pepys, as terrible as an army with banners. But life is sweet, even here in this hell on earth, foul with the pestilential breath of evil. Foh! How it stinks!

"—to the end that all godly people, hearing that bell, and knowing that it is for your going to your deaths, may be stirred up heartily to pray God to bestow his grace and mercy upon you whilst you live—" Grace and mercy indeed! Oh, sinful Sam Atkins! This is your punishment for your wicked way of life, for your fall from grace, yielding to carnal temptation. But, oh, Sally! Sally with the soft white limbs and round breasts like two young roes! Tender, loving Sally! God forgive me, a miserable sinner!

"—I beseech you, for Jesus Christ's sake, to keep this night in watching and prayer, to the salvation of your own souls, while there is yet time and place for mercy, as knowing tomorrow you must appear before the judgment seat of your creator, there to give an account of things done in this life and to suffer eternal torment for your sins committed against Him—" But surely the King would believe him, the King would save him. Sam had seen him often, a tall dark man with a saturnine face, walking at his wonted large pace through the Whitehall galleries or in St. James's Park, with courtiers trailing after him. King Charles was a good, merciful man, the father of his people. Mr. Pepys would plead for him with the King, and the King would save him from the gallows.

"—unless upon your hearty and unfeigned repentance you find mercy through the merits, death, and passion of your only mediator and advocate Jesus Christ, who now sits at the right hand of God to make intercession for as many of you as penitently return to him."

The sexton rang his handbell for the last time. Torn by grief and fear, Sam Atkins turned to his only comforter. He did not believe in miracles, but he firmly believed in the effectiveness of prayer. Kneeling by the window, he prayed long and fervently. Then he went to bed, but the grimy fingers of dawn had smudged his windows before he fell asleep.

The next day, according to plan, Lord Shaftesbury declared in a passionate speech that the only way to save the country was to dismiss the Duke of York from the Privy Council. In the following week, both Houses presented the King with addresses to that purpose. Bowing before the storm, King Charles gave in. The attack on the Duke was well under way. Now if only Sam Atkins would confess, the faction could accuse Mr. Pepys of murdering Justice Godfrey at the Duke's instigation.

On the night of Sam Atkins's arrest, Mr. Pepys, having heard nothing about the summons from a King's Messenger, expected the clerk's return after dark. At nine o'clock, when Sam had not appeared, the Secretary ordered Tom, the porter of Derby House, "to keep him out of doors in case he should come, and to tell him that his master had resolved that he should never come within his doors more." Mr. Pepys was fond of Sam, but he ran a tight ship and insisted on strict obedience. The clerk had had a second chance; he would not get a third. Half angry and half sorry, Mr. Pepys went to bed.

On Saturday morning, November 2, he caused inquiries to be made. London was a small, closely knit city, and news and rumors traveled on clacking tongues from the galleries of Whitehall to public offices, taverns, and coffeehouses. Moreover, Captain Charles Atkins was already bragging about his triumph over Sam. As Mr. Pepys himself wrote, "It appeared upon inquiry after him the next day that his absence from home overnight did not arise from any wilful failure of his, but from his being seized abroad by a messenger from Mr. Secretary Coventry upon the score of Captain Atkins's information and carried to Newgate."

When he finally had all the important facts (including, no doubt, the gist of Captain Atkins's Examination before Sir Philip Howard), Mr. Pepys was annoyed but not greatly disturbed. Captain Atkins's "information" was patently absurd; no sensible man could take it seriously. Clearly the captain was aiming at Mr. Pepys with his nonsense, but Mr. Pepys had the best alibi in the world: at the time of Godfrey's murder he had been with the King at Newmarket. Until now he had never heard of the sailor John Child.

Nevertheless, these were times of grief and fear, when no man was safe. The Secretary decided to do what he could to help his favorite clerk. With his usual vigor he set about collecting information and drawing up "An Account of Atkins' Birth, Education, and Profession as to Protestancy." In the present storm of anti-Catholic propaganda, it was important to show that Sam Atkins's "Protestancy" was a sturdy oak. Meanwhile, as insurance against charges of Popery, on Sunday, November 3, Mr. Pepys and his remaining clerks took the Anglican Sacrament at St. Margaret's Church.

In Newgate, Sam Atkins would have felt less miserable had he known of his master's concern for him. Unfortunately, Captain Richardson obeyed orders all too well; he allowed Sam no liberty, no visitors or messages, no books or writing materials. The prisoner could only pace his narrow room, gaze longingly out the window, and ruminate. He had an excellent memory. As he walked, he recalled every word spoken the night before at Winchester House, every gesture and tone of voice. He went over the dialogue again and again, searching for a way to convince the Secret Committee that he had told the truth. If he could only talk to Mr. Pepys! Wise Mr. Pepys could tell him what to do. Sam had an almost child-like faith in his master.

In a sense, Sam Atkins had led a sheltered life. He had been content with his work, his friends, an occasional outing at Vauxhall, the Spring Garden, or on the river, and the stolen sweets of taverns, playhouses, and wenches to dally with—meaning no harm. His father, his teachers, his succession of masters, and most of the merchants and naval officers he had met in the course of his duties had been men of probity and good will. Of course, he knew that there were wicked men abroad, and at night he stepped warily, his hand on his sword-hilt, for fear of footpads. No doubt, like thousands of other Londoners, he had gone at least once to see an evil-doer carted to the gallows at Tyburn, where Jack Ketch, the hangman, pushed him off the cart with a rope around his neck and left him to kick and dangle until he died. Sam remembered hearing Mr. Pepys say, "There is no pain at all in hanging, for that it do stop the circulation of the blood, and so stops all sense and motion in an instant." It was a comforting thought.

Sam knew that the world was full of evil, but until now it had not touched him; he had never walked in the way of the ungodly. By straining his imagination to the utmost he could understand how Captain Charles, pressed by his needs and tempted by the £500 reward, could become such a perfidious rogue. But how could the Secret Committee accept his lies as truth? Everyone knew that the Papists had murdered Godfrey. How could the lords believe that Sam Atkins, a true and faithful Protestant, could ever have had a part in a Jesuit plot? The lords were good, honorable gentlemen, peers of the realm—and one of them was a bishop! Surely they labored in the bog of error, and it was his duty to rescue them with the rope of reason.

The flaw in Captain Atkins's testimony was his phrase "upon this occasion," presumably the news that Godfrey was concerned in the discovery of the Popish Plot. Now if Sam could only make the lords realize that his meeting with the captain in mid-August was a good two weeks before Mr. Oates discovered the Plot—well, surely they would let him go. He could hardly have been discussing the Plot with Captain Atkins before either of them had heard about it!

When he was certain that he had his arguments well in order, Sam asked Captain Richardson to notify the Secret Committee that he had something to say. On Wednesday, November 6, a warder, Mr. Lion, took Sam to the chamber of the Lord Privy Seal in the Parliament House, where the Committee was meeting. (The quickest way to Westminster was by Old Bailey Hill and Castle Lane to Blackfriars Stairs, and thence by boat around the great bend of the Thames to Parliament Stairs.)

The Privy Seal chamber was a dignified room with a fireplace, a long table covered with green cloth, stiff-backed chairs, and tapestried walls. The lords, seated at the table, greeted Sam warmly.

"Well," said Lord Halifax, "we hope, Sam Atkins, you have considered of this business and are ready to give us some light in it." The Great Trimmer was not happy with his extremist colleagues; unlike them he had a conscience, and he did not believe that the end justified the means.

"My lord," said Sam confidently, "I have well considered of it, and I hope I am prepared to show your lordships nothing is to be expected of me, and so my liberty will not be denied me."

"Nay, then," said Lord Halifax, "you must stay till we send for Charles Atkins if you have anything to say against him and his accusations."

"My lord, I hope I shall confute him in his circumstances, which I have better considered, and clear to you my innocence."

"Why," said Lord Shaftesbury, scowling, "Charles Atkins has said he'll overturn you by other circumstances and show you the worst man living."

Sam Atkins clung to his dignity. He would not be baited into losing his temper again. "My lord," he said stiffly, "I desire, if you please, he be sent for."

A messenger was sent for Charles Atkins, who was at Sir Philip Howard's lodgings. Sam and his warder left the chamber and went downstairs to wait in the entrance passageway. Half an hour later, Captain Charles arrived; he refused to meet his victim's eyes. Perhaps it was only Sam's imagination, but it seemed to him that the captain had suddenly turned pale.

"So," said the clerk, "you can't look me in the face. Truly, I don't wonder at it. I'm glad you conscience is not quite lost." Captain Charles turned away, with Sam in pursuit. "Mr. Atkins," he said (spitefully dropping the Captain"("what, I wonder, has led you to this against me? Are you resolved to ruin me forever?"

"I? Not I," said Captain Charles, with an attempt at injured innocence.

"Do you think in your conscience I had any hand in the murder of Sir Edmund Godfrey? Do I look as if I had any design in me?"

"No, faith," said Captain Charles, "I dare swear for you for that matter, you are innocent of it. Only you know those words passed between us."

"Well, you say 'twas between us, so 'tis impossible to contradict your oath, but God, you, and I know 'twas not so."

Captain Charles muttered something under his breath, then he said aloud, "My wife asked me how you did, whether you was like to come to any harm, and I told her no, unless he brings it on himself."

Before Sam could press the captain to explain his remark, the Secret Committee summoned both men. Captain Charles took his stand at one end of the long table, Sam near the other. Confronted by the lords in all their majesty, Sam Atkins drew a deep breath and summoned up his courage.

"My lords," he said, "I desire that Charles Atkins's accusation may be read over, or else I shall repair to my memory."

"Do repair to your memory," said Lord Shaftesbury, mockingly.

Sam repeated the accusation without a slip. Then he launched into his defense. He had his arguments all in order. First he denied that there had ever been trouble between Mr. Pepys and Justice Godfrey.

"I never in my whole life heard Mr. Pepys mention Sir Edmund Godfrey's name but on an occasion of our going before him about some money lost from Mr. Pepys' house, and then they appeared as good friends as could be, and showed mutually great expressions of kindness and respect. As for Charles Atkins' positive oath about the difference 'twixt Mr. Pepys and Sir Edmund Godfrey, that will admit of no more than my denying it and being ready and desirous, if you please, to swear to the truth of what I say."

"No," said Lord Shaftesbury curtly.

Sam took the expected blow without flinching and continued, denying that he had said anything about Godfrey not being a member of Parliament, insisting that "to this minute I don't know whether he was so or no, and so could not make him that positive answer he says I did." The lords lifted incredulous eyebrows.

"Then as to the rise of the difference to be (as he calls it) 'upon this occasion,' the last time I say Mr. Atkins before Sir Edmund Godfrey's death was in August before Bartholomew Fair a little, and before the Plot was discovered, so what means he by 'upon this occasion?' Besides, I assure your lordships I did not know till after the death of Sir Edmund Godfrey that he took any depositions or was otherwise instrumental in discovering any part of the Plot."

At this the lords cried out, "What! Impossible!—You lived in an office of business and did not hear of his taking the depositions?—'Twas a whole month before the King went to Newmarket.—Aye, early in September, and carried to the Privy Council!" Taken aback by the angry chorus, Sam found himself wondering why the lords would never believe him when he was telling the truth. Would they believe him if he lied, and admitted that he was lying?

"My lords," he said, "pray suppose (what is so utterly in fact untrue) I had said to Captain Atkins what he swears I did. I must now declare I had no ground to say so, and that it must arise purely from my own invention, and if I invented a lie, I must suffer for doing it; and pray, my lords, what will come on't?"

"Nay, nay," said Shaftesbury quickly, "leave us to make the use of it. Do you but confess it. You shall be safe and we'll apply it." The lords looked up hopefully. The foolish clerk was beginning to see reason at last. As a willing witness against Mr. Pepys he would be worth a dozen paid informers. But Sam had no intention of going along with the cheat. Now he had his answer, and now was the time to twist, turn, bargain, haggle, and perhaps out-wit the Secret Committee. But there was no guile in Sam Atkins. He flushed with anger.

"My lord," he cried, "I can't do it. I hope I never shall tell a lie to any man's prejudice, though I meet with ne'er so great a danger."

"Truly, Mr. Atkins," said Lord Shaftesbury with heavy sarcasm, "are you so innocent? You're very unfortunate, and Charles Atkins the greatest villain in the world. Pray, look one another in the face.—Come, Mr. Charles Atkins, confess truly, have you belied Samuel Atkins or no? It is the same thing as to belie an emperor, for every private man is a little emperor of himself. Maybe you are mistaken. Come, Come!"

Again Sam fancied that he saw the captain turn pale and his lips lose their color. "My lords," he cried, "pray, observe his countenance changes."

"Where? Where?", said Lord Winchester. "I don't see it."

"My lord, his very appearance, I humbly conceive."

"Aye? Aye? Where?" Lord Winchester turned away, carefully seeing nothing. The other lords refused to look. Captain Atkins, who had been rolling his long clay pipe between his fingers, suddenly smashed it upon the table.

"Why should I say so, my lords," he cried, "if he had not told me?"

Sir Philip Howard spoke up warmly in his nephew's defense. Captain Atkins was a gentleman, he said, son of Sir Jonathan Atkins and otherwise well allied, and "I examined him so strictly that it was not possible he should lie."

The lords nodded gravely. Sam Atkins looked at their smug, pitiless faces and despaired. But there was the Bishop of London; perhaps he was more tender-hearted than the rest. While Captain Atkins talked to the lords at the other end of the table, Sam addressed himself to the prelate, talked about his Protestantism, and insisted that he had never seen a mass above once or twice—out of mere curiosity—and had never known a priest.

"Truly," said the bishop, "I believe you are a Protestant, but this oath is greatly against you, and Captain Atkins affirms it still positively."

"My lord," Sam protested, " 'tis strange I should invent such a lie to tell Mr. Atkins of my master. 'Tis strange I should ask Mr. Atkins of the courage and secrecy of a man I never saw, and as strange to bid him send him to my master, who will, I suppose, declare whether I ever spoke to him about any such man, as I am sure I did not. My lord, I avow to you that Mr. Pepys never in his life committed any secret to me of any kind, nor ever mentioned upon any occasion one word about Sir Edmund Godfrey. And this you'd believe if you knew how totteringly I stand in his opinion, having been turned away from him, and kept at this moment, I believe, in his very ill apprehension."

"Why," said my Lord London, "are you given to drink or debauchery?"

The bishop had touched a tender spot in Sam's conscience, but the word "given," meaning "addicted," left him room for an honest answer. "No my lord, I thank God not, but Mr. Pepys is the severest man in his house in the world, and whoever serves him laudably for seven years, for an hour's absence from his business without his knowledge shall lose his favor. Besides, I came very young to his house, and was inclined through my boyishness to too much desire of ease and liberty, and begot his very severe hand over me at first, and he has since continued it."

Lord Shaftesbury broke in, "Why, you talk! 'Twill be made appear you are the greatest favorite he has. You read all his letters, read to him o' nights, and 'twill be proved you are reputed a Catholic in your house."

"Do that," said Sam quickly, "and I'll plead no more."

Shaftesbury refused the gambit. "Pray," he said, "what books used you to read to him?"

"Sir, I have not lately read to him at all, but I used to read the Bible and other good books, sometimes history, other times divinity."

"Never any Popish books?"

"Never in my life, I assure your lordship, never any. But, as I remember one book containing several disputes and confutations upon and to their doctrine and religion—particularly about their error in the Doctrine of Transubstantiation—but I remember not the book's name."

There was no more to be said. The Committee had gained nothing from Sam, nor Sam from the Committee, in spite of his rope of reason. His plea for liberty on bail was brusquely denied. The fly was in the web; let him struggle and tire himself out. The Committee granted one request: Sam Atkins's sister was given leave to visit him—just once—with Captain Richardson present at the interview.

Sam journeyed back to Newgate with a heavy heart. Now he knew that the lords were not honorable gentlemen; they were Godless men. Like Worldly Wiseman in Mr. Bunyan's *Pilgrim's Progress*, they dwelt in the town of Carnal Policy. They actually wanted him to lie, to accuse his master, Mr. Pepys. Good God, what an age is this and what a world is this, that a man cannot live without playing the knave and dissimulation! Sam was too sunk in his own misery to see that he was merely a pawn blocking Shaftesbury's scheme to checkmate the Duke of York.

On Thursday, November 7, Captain Richardson brought Sam's sister to him and stayed in his room for the "half a quarter of an hour" allowed for her visit. The Secret Committee was not being generous in permitting her visit. Captain Richardson took mental notes of everything the prisoner said, hoping that in his excitement he would let slip an admission of guilt, or say something which could be used to force a confession from him. But Sam had time only to reassure his sister about his health and explain his need for money to pay his daily charges in Newgate. In turn, his sister could only tell him that his friends were doing everything they could for him. Then the Keeper took her away, and Sam was alone again in his dreary cell.

Early the next morning, Friday, November 8, Captain Richardson brought Charles Atkins into Sam's room while the prisoner was still in bed. As the Keeper turned to leave Sam leaped out of bed in his shirt, crying, "Hold, captain, a word with you." At the door he begged, "For God's sake, don't leave me alone with this man. He'll possibly go and swear God knows what against me as he has already done."

"The lords have ordered he must be alone with you," said Captain Richardson.

"Oh? Pray, don't suffer it. I wont speak a word to him alone."

"I'll come up to you immediately," said the Keeper. He closed the door, and Sam heard his descending footsteps.

Captain Atkins was the picture of woe. Tears stood in his eyes and he wrung his hands. "Oh, Sam Atkins," he moaned, "we are both undone."

"How undone?"

"There's a man came last night who was examined two hours by the King and has sworn positively against you, that you were at the murder of Sir Edmund Godfrey."

"Well, God bless him," said Sam wearily. "But how are you undone? 'Tis I am so, if this be true."

"Why," said Captain Charles, weeping and laying his hand on his breast, "I am undone."

"That's true; your guilt has undone you. But, pray, who is this man? Do you know him?"

"I don't know his name nor ever saw him but once, and that was in Essex building. The woman of a house was arrested where we were, and he and I rescued her from the bailiffs."

"Well, I can't help what he has done. I thank you for all this. I don't doubt if twenty swear against me, I shall appear innocent in the last moment of my life."

"Pray, Sam Atkins, consider of it," the captain pleaded. "My uncle, Phil Howard, bid me come to tell you of it, and pray confess before 'tis too late and you regret you did not. There is nothing can hurt you, but your fortune may be made by it. And what need you care for your master?"

"Ask me to forego my salvation. A thousand deaths shall not extort a lie from me, and you know I can say nothing." Once more Sam went over old ground; he did not know Child, and he had never said a word to Captain Charles about Mr. Pepys and Justice Godfrey.

"You did not tell me neither," said Captain Charles viciously, "that your master had a house at Rouen in France, did you?" The implication that Mr. Pepys was a crypto-Catholic was obvious.

"Oh, God! Why, have you sworn that too?"

"No, not I. What should I swear it for?" The threat was thinly veiled. "But you told me so. You know you desired me to impeach your master about this murder because he should keep it off from the Duke of York."

"Oh, Lord of Heaven!" Sam was overwhelmed. "And have you sworn that too?"

"No, not I. I shan't swear it. What for? But you know you told me so."

For a moment Sam was close to an understanding of Lord Shaftesbury's plot against the Duke, but he was too overcome to follow up the captain's leads and get the whole story. He could hardly believe his ears. Like the foul fiend, the captain told his atrocious lies with a perfectly straight face. "This is the greatest wonder and miracle of wickedness that ever I saw," Sam groaned, sinking back against the side of his bed.

Again Captain Charles urged him to confess, promising that if he joined in the captain's "information" he would have a great reward. "Being young men," he said, "we ought to lay hold on this fair occasion of making our fortunes."

"Mr. Atkins," said Sam, "you are the greatest villain and worst man in the world—"

Captain Charles interrupted him. "Consider of it against the afternoon," he said gloomily, "when you'll be called for, I believe, to the Committee of Lords." He left the room without a farewell, and Sam Atkins could only guess about his villainous designs.

Almost hidden among Captain Atkins's lies was a single fact: an informer had been examined the day before. At Bristol, an old acquaintance of Titus Oates, "Captain" William Bedloe, a swindler, imposter, thief, and sharper, had heard about the reward for the discovery of Godfrey's killers and had hurried to London. On Thursday afternoon, before the King and the two Secretaries of State, he had deposed that he knew nothing about the Popish Plot, but that in October two Jesuits, named Le Faire and Pritchard, had offered him £4,000 to help murder Godfrey. Of course he had refused, indignantly. He learned later, he said, that on the night of October 14, Godfrey had been smothered with a pillow in the Queen's residence, Somerset House. The murderers were Le Faire, another Jesuit named Walsh, a gentleman in the service of the Catholic Lord Bellasis, "and the youngest of the waiters in the Queen's Chapel, in a purple gown." Bedloe had *not* named Sam Atkins.

But on Friday morning, even while Captain Charles was browbeating his victim in Newgate, Captain Bedloe was repeating his sensational story at the bar of the House of Lords, with additions and changes so significant that the King mused, "Surely this man has received a new lesson during the last twenty-four hours." He had indeed. Now Bedloe knew almost as much about the Popish Plot as Oates himself—enough so that he could serve as the necessary second witness in trials for high treason. Having learned overnight that Godfrey had been strangled, he changed his information: Godfrey, he said, was first stifled with a pillow and then strangled with a long cravat.

Bedloe repeated the story that he had been offered £4,000 to help murder Godfrey. Then he deposed that, at about half past eight on the night of Monday, October 14, he had met Le Faire at Somerset House and learned that Godfrey was dead. Now Le Faire offered him £2,000 to help dispose of the body. His helpers would be Le Faire, Walsh, Lord Bellasis's servant, an unnamed servant of the Chapel whom Bedloe had often seen, and "Mr. Atkins, Pepys's clerk."

Le Faire led Bedloe into a room in sprawling Somerset House. There, revealed by a shaft of light from a dark lantern, lay Godfrey's body, and about it stood his slayers, one of whom owned himself to be "Mr. Atkins, Pepys's clerk." Clearly someone had told Bedloe to include Sam Atkins in his lurid testimony.

Captain Charles must have known in advance what Bedloe was going to say Friday morning to the House of Lords. An easy explanation is that the two rogues, Captain Charles and Bedloe, cooked up the story between them. In spite of the captain's disclaimer, they were old acquaintances, and since coming to London Bedloe lodged where Captain Charles lived, near Wild House. But this theory ignores Captain Charles's heartfelt "Why, I am undone," and his desperate attempt to get Sam to go along with his own "information."

Surely Lord Shaftesbury, or someone else on the Secret Committee, told Bedloe to bring Sam Atkins into his fantastic yarn. Sir Philip Howard, almost constantly with the Committee, would have warned his nephew that Bedloe was about to steal his thunder and his chance at a goodly share of the £500 reward. Captain Charles, a mere dabbler as an informer, hastened to Newgate to try to persuade Sam, with a mixture of pleas and threats, to confess before it was too late—too late, that is, for Captain Charles's hopes of the reward.

Certainly Bedloe's new "information" was just what Lord Shaftesbury needed. Now he could squeeze Sam Atkins dry and bully him into indicting Mr. Pepys. Then (as Roger North said), "through Mr. Pepys, by like process of threats and promises (for he was an elderly gentleman [he was forty-five!] who had known softness and the pleasures of life), they might have that murder charged on the Duke of York. For Mr. Pepys, in desperate circumstances, might be as likely to accuse the Duke as his man Atkins was to accuse him."

Lord Shaftesbury conjured up delightful pictures of Mr. Pepys in irons, cowering before the Secret Committee and incriminating the Duke of York in Godfrey's murder. With an accessory charge against him, the Duke would be lucky to escape with permanent exile. King Charles would have to name a new heir—his oldest natural son, James Duke of Monmouth, or his nephew, William of Orange— and Shaftesbury would become the power behind the throne. The fate of nations depended on the weakness or strength of an Admiralty clerk.

Of course, Sam Atkins had no inkling of the dark designs and stratagems of the Secret Committee. On Friday afternoon, as Captain Charles had predicted, Sam was loaded with irons, thrust into a coach, and carried along Fleet Street, the Strand, and King Street to the Parliament House. The day was foggy and cold, and the coach shutters were closed; but Sam could hear the familiar clatter of traffic, the jingling of carriers' bells, and the cries of street vendors: "Mackerel, four for sixpence"—"Oysters twelve pence a peck"—"New River Water"—"Small coals, small coals!" A wave of nostalgia and self-pity overcame him. He longed for his tavern friends, his fellow clerks, even the scolding of Mr. Pepys and Mr. Hewer. Tears fell upon his manacles.

After a long wait, Sam was called up to the Lord Privy Seal's chamber, where he found the Secret Committee in full force, with John Wildman, the famous republican, as secretary. The high gothic windows were tightly closed against the fog; candles and the glow of a sea-coal fire brightened the room.

Behind the lords at the table stood a tall, dignified gentleman with a military coat, a basket-hilted sword, and a black periwig. He had a harsh, deeply lined face, heavy black brows, and a protruding nether lip. He came forward, saluted Sam, and returned to his place.

"Do you know this gentleman?" asked Lord Shaftesbury.

"No, my lord," Sam replied, "I never saw him in my life that I remember."

"I believe I have seen you somewhere," the gentleman said, "but I can't tell where. I don't know; I can't remember where."

"Is this the man?" barked the Duke of Buckingham, pointing at Sam Atkins.

"My lord, I can't swear this is he." The informer was cautious; he was a newcomer to the game and, out of sheer ignorance, he had already made some bad mistakes. It was always possible that his victim might have an alibi. " 'Twas a young man, and he told me his name was Atkins, a clerk belonging to Derby House. He is in all things very like the person I saw in the room with Sir Edmund Bury Godfrey's dead body, and I do verily believe it was he that owned himself to be Pepys' clerk, but because I never saw him before that time, I can't positively swear it."

Before Sam could recover from the shock of the accusation, the Secret Committee turned on him, demanding to know where he had been on Monday, October 14, between nine and ten o'clock at night. Still dazed, Sam confessed that he did not know, he could not remember. "I suppose at home, for I am seldom out at that time of night."

"Were you in the Pall Mall, or that way, that you remember?" St. James's Palace was at the end of Pall Mall.

"No, my lord, I believe verily not." On the spur of the moment, who can remember where he has been a month ago?

Shaftesbury dismissed the informer and turned grimly to Sam Atkins. "Mr. Atkins," he said, "if you are innocent you are the most unfortunate wretch alive. I'll tell you what—here is good news for you—here's but one way to save your life, and you may now have it. Confess all you know and make a discovery in this matter, and your life will be saved."

Sam protested his innocence at length—brevity was not one of his virtues—and concluded with a ringing defiance, "I would rather suffer a thousand deaths than tell a solemn lie to the prejudice of anybody."

Lord Shaftesbury heard him out. He was wise in the weaknesses of men and could tolerate foolish heroics. But it was time to let this irritating clerk know what was in store for him.

"I'll tell you what," he said sharply, "you'll be hanged— which I never told you before—or knighted. If the Papists rise and cut our throats, you'll be knighted; if not, you'll be hanged. Here's first what you said to Captain Atkins, and now this man's oath against you, which, though not positive, is so circumstantial as I doubt whether a jury in this case won't find you guilty. Consider what collateral circumstances may be brought in. And another thing, here are other persons who are known to this Mr. Bedloe to have been concerned in it—"

"And who are in the house," said Buckingham.

"—and if one of them swears you were in it, all the world can't save you."

Sam Atkins's body was weak with fear, but his spirit was still strong. "My lord," he said unsteadily, "my prayers are and shall be to God Almighty that but one person may be detected who was really accessory, and I am sure I shall be acquitted, and I cannot suffer but from the matter's being misplaced."

"Oh, he'll confess nothing," Buckingham sneered. "He expects a pardon."

Lord Shaftesbury, thinking of the Opposition power in Parliament, said confidently, "I'll secure him from that. There's three hundred to one." Only the King could pardon a convicted felon, and with revolution in the air, and his people mad with fear, the King was helpless.

Sam Atkins had the last word. "My lord, I expect no pardon, but desire death when I am found to deserve it. I have nothing to trust to but my innocence and the goodness of God Almighty, to whom I commit myself."

Sam traveled the long cold road back to prison, convinced that he was as good as dead. The God-fearing members of the Secret Committee sent word to Captain Richardson to keep the clerk in irons and to throw him in with other prisoners for greater security and the full flavor of Newgate. If that failed—well, there was always the condemned hole, a dark, freezing, airless cell, deep underground. Sooner or later Sam Atkins would break.

On Saturday, November 9, the jailers loaded Sam Atkins
with shackles, turned him out of his room in the Head
Keeper's lodgings, and took him to the entrance lodge for
reassignment. By paying a heavy fee he secured a chamber
in the Press Yard, the aristocratic section of Newgate.

The Press Yard, three floors high, was between the Felons'
Side and the Debtors' Side, and had an enclosure where the
prisoners could walk in the open air. Unfortunately, Sam
was confined to his cell. The weekly rent for a room was
eleven shillings and sixpence, and the prisoner had to provide
his own food, fuel, lights, and drinks. Throughout the prison
were various drinking cellars and tap rooms, where wine
was sold at two shillings a bottle, ale at fourpence a quart,
and brandy at fourpence a quartern (a quarter of a pint).
The profits went to Captain Richardson, of course.

The first night Sam got very little sleep. His cell was cold
in spite of a charcoal brazier; his irons were a constant
torment; he was bitten by fleas and bedbugs; and his ears
were assailed by bedlam.

Ordinarily the Felons' Master Side and the Felons'
Common Side were filled with the dregs of London awaiting trial (or, if convicted, the gallows) for such capital
crimes as high and petty treason, coining, murder, man-
slaughter, rape, arson, burglary, highway robbery, and the
theft of goods worth a shilling or more. Usually, too, there
were many lesser culprits charged with perjury, forgery,
mayhem, sodomy, assault, petty theft, or beggary, and
destined for the pillory, the whipping post, or the cart's

tail. Now in addition, jammed into cells, the common rooms, and the condemned hole, there were dozens of priests and Catholic laymen accused of complicity in the Popish Plot, and even a few unfortunates suspected of having had a hand in Godfrey's murder—notably the two men who had found his body, William Bromwell, a baker, and John Walters, a blacksmith. The normal night noises of Newgate multiplied—the sounds of revelry, drunken brawls, bellows of rage, screams, curses, and maudlin songs. To the uproar inside the prison was added the howling of vengeful Protestants outside the walls.

The London mobs wanted blood. Nearly a month had passed since Godfrey's death, and the leaders of the faction who now controlled Parliament still hesitated to bring anyone to trial for his murder. With Bedloe's evidence, Sam Atkins was their best prospect, but the hue and cry could not find the two Jesuits, Le Faire and Walsh, or Lord Bellasis's gentleman, or the mysterious chapel keeper in his purple gown. As evidence against Mr. Pepys's clerk, the lords had both Bedloe's deposition (but not his oath) and Captain Charles Atkins's testimony, but the discrepancy between the two accounts was glaring. If only the stubborn clerk would confess!

On the morning of Monday, November 11, Captain Charles visited Sam Atkins in his cold, dreary cell, bade him a cheerful good morrow, asked how he did, and inquired if he had been before the Secret Committee of lords.

"Yes," said Sam. His irons were no heavier than his spirits. "I saw a man there—I know not whom—nor he me—nor did he swear anything against me."

Captain Charles lighted his new pipe and smoked furiously. The prison stench was particularly bad that morning. "Aye," he said, "but he swore in the House of Commons on Saturday night that you were at Somerset House with Sir Edmund Godfrey's body, and my uncle, Phil Howard, bade me come to tell you of it, that you may consider and confess all you know before it is too late."

Sam was too sunk in misery to reply with his usual warmth. "Well," he sighed, "my last breath will agree with what I said at first, of my not being able to say anything of this whole matter than an unborn child. Pray, who is this man?"

"Why, his name is Bedloe."

"Is he a man of any good fame?"

"No, no very good fame."

"Do you know him?"

"Yes, I have known him three or four months, no very great acquaintance with him, and I don't believe a word he says. 'Tis all shams. He is certainly hired by those who did it."

"Do you think so?"

"Aye, aye," said Captain Charles. "Trouble not yourself. But I believe you'll be called again today before the lords."

"Well, what they please."

Captain Charles realized that he could get nothing from the clerk in his despondent mood. He left in a cloud of tobacco smoke, and Sam had another puzzle. He remembered that earlier the captain had said he did not know Bedloe; now he said he had known him three or four months. Earlier the captain had been shaken by the appearance of a second informer; now he was belittling Bedloe's evidence—" 'Tis all shams." Something had happened between the two liars. Sam Atkins's lips twisted into a wry smile as he remembered the old adage "Two of a trade never agree." He took no comfort from the thought; when the two scoundrels gave their testimony in court, they would agree well enough to hang him.

On Tuesday morning, November 12, Sam Atkins, led by a jailer, clanked downstairs to a room in the Keeper's lodgings where a committee from the House of Commons awaited him: Mr. William Sacheverel, Sergeant-at-law William Gregory, Colonel John Birch, and Sir Gilbert Gerard—all members of the Opposition Party. Sam recognized only Colonel Birch, a tough old Puritan who had begun life as a carrier and had risen to the rank of colonel in the Roundhead Army. Sam's dead hopes flickered into life. Surely Colonel Birch, a man of the people and a good Protestant, would believe him. Unfortunately the colonel was one of Mr. Pepys's bitterest enemies.

The members wasted no time. Dwelling first upon the enormity of Sam's crime, they told him that his situation was desperate, and that he could save his life only by a complete confession. "What do you have to say, Mr. Atkins?"

"I heartily wish I could give you any light in this matter," Sam replied in his most formal style. "I should deem myself very happy to be enabled to acquit myself of the duty I owe to his Majesty, but I am purely innocent, and whatever was sworn against me might with the same truth be sworn against anyone."

Mr. Sacheverel, Shaftesbury's jackal in the Commons, pursed his lips scornfully. He was already convinced of Sam's guilt. "Do you know anyone named Welsh or Walsh, or one named Pritchard?"

"No, nor ever heard of them that I remember."

"Do you remember anything about Monday, October 14, and a dark lantern?"

"No, sir."

"Were you not at Somerset House then?"

"I was never in the house in my life, and but once in the chapel, three or four years since."

"Where did you spend your time that Saturday, Sunday, and Monday?"

"I can't presently tell, but I can soon recollect myself."

"What, were you not at church Sunday?"

"No, sir."

The gentlemen shook their heads sadly. What was the younger generation coming to? "Do you know nothing at all about Sir Edmund Godfrey's murder or the Plot?"

"No, sir, I do not."

Finally the gentlemen took their leave, one saying sadly, "So, you are resolved to deny all." Reporting later to the House of Commons, Mr. Sacheverel said, "I must needs say this much of Atkins, that he is as ingenious a man to say nothing as ever I heard."

Sam Atkins shuffled back to his cell more depressed than ever. No one would believe him. But at least he had learned something. The Secret Committee of lords had asked him where he was on October 14, between nine and ten at night. Now the gentlemen from the House of Commons wanted him to account for his time for three days: October 12 through 14, but especially for Monday the fourteenth. Sam remembered hearing Mr. Bedloe say that on the night of October 14 he had seen at Somerset House one who called himself Atkins, a clerk at Derby House. Clearly Sam must remember where he had been during those three days. He sat down and tried to think.

October 12—wasn't that the day of Godfrey's disappearance? Sam remembered a conversation with his fellow clerk John Walbanke, the following Monday morning—Monday, October 14.

"Poor Sir Edmund Godfrey," said Walbanke.

"Why?" Sam asked, "What's the matter with him?"

"Why they say he is murdered by the Papists, having been gone from his house and not found this day or two."

"Come, why should he be murdered, a good, honest gentleman?"

"Aye, but it seems he was the first man to take the depositions about the plot."

Had Sam talked to anyone else that morning? Laboriously he reconstructed the day hour by hour, remembering the work he had done, the visitors to Derby House, and the officers who had come to report or to receive orders—Captain Roydon, Lieutenant Harris, Captain Moone, Captain Vittles—Captain Vittles! That was the day when—

In a blinding flash the whole picture was complete in all its horror. Sam Atkins groaned aloud and bowed his head to his manacled hands. The shameful memories he had been trying so long to deny or to transform into the remnants of a nightmare came back to him in quick vignettes. First came the climax early on Tuesday morning:

Sally clutching the sheet to her naked breasts—the outraged face and bitter scolding of his landlady, Mrs. Bulstrode, with the wide-eyed maid peering over her shoulder—his own stammering, half-awake excuses. Oh, God! He was never so shamed in all his life! He hated to think what it had cost him in protests and promises (plus a shilling to the maid) before he could get the intruders out of his room so that Sally could dress in guilty haste and slip down to the street door.

Monday afternoon came next to his anguished mind: the gay trip down-river with Sally Williams and her sister Anne—the King's yacht—Captain Vittle's expansive hospitality—the yacht's little cabin with its red velvet cushions —laughter and dallying and wine—Oh, God, the wine! If ever he was soundly foxed!

Then came the boat ride up-river to the bridge late at night—the coach, with himself half asleep—Sally's kisses and whispers—Sally naked in bed—the way of a man with a maid! Drunkenness and fornication! God forgive a miserable sinner!

But the date had been Monday, October 14, of that fact Sam was positive. Resolutely he banished visions and vain regrets; what was done was done, and the hand of God was heavy upon him for his iniquities. Now to go back and reconstruct the weekend.

Mr. Pepys had left for Newmarket on Friday, October 11. Saturday morning Mrs. Bulstrode's maid had wakened Sam at his usual early hour. He had taken his morning draught of small beer at a nearby tavern and had arrived at Derby House at eight o'clock as usual. He had dined at his lodgings—Mrs. Bulstrode set a good table—and then— Oh, thou wicked and slothful servant!—he had taken advantage of Mr. Pepys's absence to divert himself with vain pleasures. He had met his good friend Captain David Lloyd at the Blue Posts in the Haymarket, had gone with him to the Drury Lane playhouse, and thence, when the play was over, to the New Exchange, where he had engaged to take the Williams sisters on an outing the following

Monday. (He knew that Mr. Pepys would not be back until Thursday.) Thereafter—aye, it was all coming back—he had gone to a tavern with John Walbanke and had drunk with him until nigh one o'clock Sunday morning.

On Sunday he had slept late. He had wakened with a headache—the wine, no doubt—and had spent most of the day at home. If only he had gone to church and taken the Sacrament! From mid-afternoon until one or two o'clock Monday morning he had been scouring the town with Captain Lloyd and his fellow clerks, Lawrence and Walbanke, ending up at the Rose Tavern in Covent Garden. Monday morning he had gone to work at his usual time. Then came Captain Vittles and his invitation to visit the yacht *Katherine.* After that—Oh, God! Sam could hardly bear to think of what he had done, yet, even as he wrestled with sinful memory, the demon in his loins awoke and flooded his veins with carnal longing. Sam Atkins was a normal young man with healthy appetites.

So he had an alibi for the night of October 14. But what would Mr. Pepys say? Sam knew very well what he would do. If he ever heard the full story of his clerk's crimes, he would dismiss him at once, without a character. Sam would have no friends and no money; his small stock of guineas was dwindling daily with the costs of Newgate for fees, food, and fuel. His training had all been in the business of the Navy; now that service and all other branches of the government would be closed to him. No merchant would hire him without a character, and he was too old to become an apprentice to another trade. At least he could enlist before the mast—the pull of the sea was strong—and become a common sailor at twenty-four shillings a month, living on weevily biscuit, dried peas, salt beef, stale beer, and water green in the cask. But he could never become an officer, not even a warrant officer. Mr. Pepys's displeasure would follow him to the ends of the earth.

The more Sam brooded, the sharper became the horns of his dilemma. Even if he could save his life by offering alibis for the fatal three days, he would be ruined, his career destroyed, and his life brought to wretchedness, misery, and an early death by plague, scurvy, fever, or an enemy bullet. If he offered no alibi, he faced death at the hands of Jack Ketch, the hangman. Which should it be, Jack Ketch or Jack Tar?

But would even an alibi save him? Sam Atkins knew, and had himself subscribed to, the accepted principle that it was better for the innocent to suffer than for the guilty to go free. He knew enough about the practice of law courts to realize that he would have to face a battery of the King's prosecutors without the help of counsel. The mere fact that he had been accused of a crime would prepossess a jury against him. He would not even know in detail what he was charged with until he faced his accusers in court, where he could only ask them questions. Confined as he was in Newgate, how could he get witnesses to support his alibis? Indeed, even if he could subpoena them, would his friends testify in the face of Mr. Pepys's displeasure?

Lost in despair, Sam Atkins reverted to the Puritan stoicism of his youth. Like the early Christians who went serenely forth to the lions' jaws, he accepted his fate and prepared himself for death. As he wrote later, "When I first came into my chamber [in the Press Yard] on Tuesday, November 8, I recollected myself where I had been that Saturday, Sunday, and Monday in October, and in half an hour I perfectly got to memory almost every hour of each day. That done, I banished all further thoughts of the matter, and I think till the 21st of November it hardly ever came into my mind, or if it did I would not suffer it to have rest there; so as I employed my time in reading, praying, and confessing my sins—work enough for one life indeed—and promised myself a dissolution of this body in a few days." Nevertheless, at night there were thoughts that nature gave way to in repose.

On November 14, Captain Richardson took pity on Sam, accepted his easement fee, and struck off his irons. The chaplain of Newgate, "the ordinary," lent him a Bible, and Sam Atkins, cherishing every word as a pearl dropped from Heaven, read it over and over. He was particularly struck by a passage in David's one hundred and ninth psalm, which he resolved to have as the text of his funeral sermon:

Hold not thy peace, O God of my praise;

For the mouth of the wicked and the mouth of the deceit-
ful are opened against me; they have spoken against me
with a lying tongue.

They compassed me about also with words of hatred, and
fought against me without cause.

For my love they are my adversaries; but I give myself
unto prayer.

And they have rewarded me evil for good, and hatred for
my love.

There was a certain morbid pleasure in being able to declare one's innocence even after death.

Kept in solitary confinement and deprived of all news from the outside world, Sam Atkins had no way of knowing that his master was moving heaven and earth to save him from Jack Ketch. When he heard about Bedloe's testimony, Mr. Pepys was seriously alarmed. He had dealt with too many rogues not to recognize Bedloe as an arrant rascal; but these were dangerous times, and normally sober Englishmen had lost their senses. Fear had made them credulous.

As a member of the Court party in the House of Commons, Mr. Pepys had noted with consternation the violence and fury of the dominant faction. He could not object to their petition that all Papists be disarmed and banished at least ten miles from London—a petition the King accepted and enforced by proclamation—but he was appalled by the Commons' new Test Act to deprive all Catholics of their seats in Parliament, even Catholic peers. Clearly this bill, now pending in the House of Lords, was aimed at Pepys's patron, the Duke of York.

Mr. Pepys realized that he too was in danger; the tagging of the man Bedloe claimed he had seen standing beside Godfrey's body as "Pepys's clerk" was no accident. Mr.

Pepys was well aware that he had many enemies in the Opposition party, and that his own fate was linked with his clerk's.

By November 14 Mr. Pepys had completed his "Account of Atkins' Birth, Education, and Profession as to Protestancy," and was investigating the clerk's activities during the crucial period, October 12 through 14. Sam Atkins had left a broad trail. His fellow clerks could testify to his time spent at Derby House and at various taverns. His landlady, Mrs. Bulstrode, and her maid could say when, how long, and with whom he had slept at home. But Mr. Pepys wanted to nail down every hour in the three days with reliable evidence given under oath.

On Saturday, November 16, he wrote to Captain David Lloyd, whose ship, the *Reserve,* was now in the Downs, being readied for a long voyage. At some length he set forth the situation and explained why he needed information about how Sam Atkins had spent his three days. He already knew (he said) that the delinquent had "employed the opportunity given him for it by that absence of mine [at Newmarket] in entertaining himself more than, had I been present, he either could or durst to have attempted."

For the present, at least, Mr. Pepys was willing to overlook Sam's offense and to deal with the more serious question of "how far he stands truly chargeable, or excusable, in this much more detestable wickedness that is laid to him of having his hand in blood." He had heard that Captain Lloyd had been much with Sam Atkins on that week-end, "particularly at the New Exchange" on Saturday and at the Rose Tavern on Sunday night, "where there was said to have happened a kind of quarrel between you and another of the company." It seems, too, that on Monday morning Sam Atkins and others had "accompanied you down to the waterside when you went down last to take boat to your ship." Therefore, would Captain Lloyd be so kind as to recollect, write down, and swear to an exact account of those three days and nights with Sam Atkins—"how, with whom, on what occasions, by what length of stays, with what discourse, action, accident, or any other circumstance relating to your being together."

With the wisdom of a veteran, Mr. Pepys cautioned Captain Lloyd to be sure that anything he wrote was the exact truth. Detection in one mistake, he pointed out, "will justly call in question the whole of what you shall say that is true." He concluded with an appeal for haste, "it being discoursed that he will be brought to trial upon Thursday next," November 21.

Captain Lloyd responded nobly, and Mr. Pepys thought his testimony so important that he persuaded the King to postpone the captain's voyage. A statement from Captain Richard Vittles, who had temporarily commanded the *Katherine* yacht, and with whom Sam Atkins and his guests had spent Monday from 4:30 in the afternoon until 10:30 at night, would be even more important. The Secretary sent word to Captain Vittles, now at Chatham, ordering him to come to Derby House at the King's expense and to bring with him the seamen from the *Katherine* who had set Sam and his guests ashore that night. From them, and from Sam's landlady, Mr. Pepys learned the rest of the story. Now he could account for his clerk's movements from Saturday morning until Tuesday morning of the fateful week-end.

The Secretary's comments on Sam's moral turpitude are not recorded. Perhaps he remembered times in his own youth when he had been coltishly amorous, and occasions when he had been "soundly foxed" by wine. He should have remembered the times when he had gone to bed with Betty Martin in her husband's absence, or with pretty Mrs. Bagwell, the navy carpenter's wife, or that day in March, 1668, when he took Betty Martin's sister, Doll Lane, to a room in the Dog Tavern, and (in his own words) "je did hazer what I did desire with her and did it backwards not having convenience to do it the other way." If he remembered, he saw no reason to be more lenient with the follies of youth. Of course Mr. Pepys had his mistress, Mary Skinner, but he was no longer coltish. Age brings discretion, a very poor substitute for youth.

Unaware that his sins had been discovered, Sam Atkins in Newgate remained in "a good, quiet posture," seeing "the hand of God in the judgment and the wrath I have pulled (as it were) from him by my iniquity." He was thinking of confessing all his sins at the gallows, and showing himself to the multitude as "the example God should make of all such rebels to the Gospel as I have been."

Early on Tuesday morning, November 19, a warder, Mr. Lion, came in to announce that Sam was to be tried that day.

"Lord," said Sam, "I wonder I had no notice of it. I have no witnesses ready."

"I don't know," said the warder, "I can't help it. You must go."

Sam got out of bed and dressed. Mr. Lion clamped his wrists in manacles fastened to a great iron bar and left the room. For two hours the stoical clerk sat and waited, "prepared to go without the least fear or discord within, but with great quiet, expecting the sentence of death." Then the warder returned.

"Hold," he said, "I am mistaken. 'Tis not for you, but for one Mr. Staley, who is to be arraigned at the Court of the King's Bench. Your trial is tomorrow." He removed the irons. If all this bustle and preparation was not an honest mistake but an attempt to frighten Sam into a confession, it failed of its purpose. Nevertheless, he lived thereafter as if each day were to be his last on earth.

The morrow came, but no summons for Sam Atkins. On Thursday, November 21—the day of Mr. Staley's trial—Sam had visitors, his sister and Mr. Pepys's solicitor, John Hayes. There were kisses, handshakes, a few tears, and a babble of excited talk. For two weeks Sam had not seen a friendly face. His joy at seeing his sister again was dampened by Mr. Hayes's account of Bedloe's testimony before Parliament. Captain Bedloe, said Hayes, was great with the leaders of the faction; his word was gospel, and the London mobs were howling for Sam's blood. There was little hope for his life.

"I do not expect it," said Sam, "I have prepared for the change as well as I can."

His friends were doing everything possible for his defense. Mr. Hayes showed him the paper drawn up by Mr. Pepys and labeled "The Method of Sam: Atkins' Defense." It was divided into four parts: first, an account of Sam's education and religion; second, a detailed statement of how he had spent the important three days; third, an account of "his accusers' lives and reputations;" and fourth, proof that what they had said about him was false.

Sam was shocked to learn that all his iniquities had been laid bare. His face burned when he came to the crucial items:

> To prove how he spent Monday
> in the afternoon from 2 o'clock
> to 12 at night.
>
> Mrs. Bulstrode
> her maid
> Mr. Manning
> Mrs. Anne Williams
> Mrs. Sarah Williams
> Mr. Harris
> Captain Vittles and
> his boatswain
> Wm. French, Rich. Dickson, Geo. Stephenson,
> the waterman, the porter
> and coachman, if to be
> found, and the waterman that carried them
> down.

Henry Pierce, waterman in
Christ Church parish over
against the Temple.

To prove he lay at home
Monday night.

Mrs. Sarah Williams
Mrs. Bulstrode
her maid.

There it all was for anybody to see and understand. The paper agreed with Sam's own recollection and differed in no essential details. Mr. Pepys had cut Sam's knotty problem with the sharp sword of evidence.

Mr. Pepys had insisted that in his defense Sam should give a complete account of Captain Atkins's surrender to the Algerines. In addition, he had found some witnesses willing to discredit that perfidious gentleman. The captain's former landlord in Drury Lane, his present landlady near Wild House, and the chirurgeon who had treated him for the pox, were all ready to testify to "his manner of living and indigency, and his usual profane swearing and wicked loose life." Two sober merchants were ready to swear to the captain's "confession of hoping to be pardoned or at least to get his bond back by this accusation" against Sam Atkins. What a precious knave he was! And one lieutenant Hord was ready to testify that Bedloe was an even more pernicious scoundrel.

Yet the Secret Committee believed both Captain Atkins and Captain Bedloe! Truly, Sam thought, "Thine enemies shall be found liars unto thee." Sam's trial, said Mr. Hayes, would take place in a day or two; he should consider well what he would say in court. And so the visitors left.

There had been no word from Mr. Pepys; no doubt he was furious. Sam took some comfort from the fact that the Secretary was working to save him from the gallows, but he suspected that Mr. Pepys, who loved justice, would do as much for anyone unjustly accused. At least Sam knew that he was not alone.

Roused from his stoic lethargy, he considered his situation again. If his witnesses could be brought into court—and he could trust Mr. Pepys and Mr. Hayes to summon them—his alibi for October 14 would clear him of Bedloe's charge—if, that is, a jury could be persuaded by an alibi which, while placing him miles from the scene of the murder, would prove him a dissolute, drunken wretch. Sometimes a jury convicted a man simply because of his ill character. Then there was still Captain Atkins's information, a charge, in effect, that Sam had helped bring Mr. Pepys and John Child together, to the end that Child, and probably some others, would murder Justice Godfrey. Bedloe's testimony made Sam a principal in the murder; Captain Atkins's information made him an accessory. In either case the penalty was death. The outlook still seemed hopeless.

But Sam Atkins's stubborn spirit came to the rescue again. His career was ruined, but, by heaven, he would make a fight for his life! For a few shillings Captain Richardson gave Sam the liberty of the prison and provided him with pen, ink, and paper. He set to work at once, writing out a complete account of his comings and goings on the days in question—but surely without confessing that he had danced the shaking of the sheets with wanton Sally! This account, supported by witnesses, would be the best means to prove his innocence, "which," he said, "is clear as noonday, and shall appear so to the minute of my death."

That done, he wrote a long, carefully detailed account of everything that had happened since his arrest on the night of November 1—everything his inquisitors had said to him, and everything he had said to them. He concluded his "Account" with a passionate declaration of his innocence, and signed the document "in the presence of the great God of Heaven, to whom be glory and praise for ever."

Even while he was writing, a Westminster grand jury was finding a true bill against him, not as an accessory to the murder of Sir Edmund Godfrey, but as the principal. "Thou, Samuel Atkins," the jurors declared, "together with——Welch and——Le Faire, gentlemen, not having the fear of God before your eyes, but being moved and seduced by the instigation of the devil, the twelfth day of October, in the thirtieth year of the reign of our sovereign lord Charles II, in and upon Sir Edmund Bury Godfrey did make an assault, and thou the said Samuel Atkins a certain linen cravat of the value of one penny about the neck of the said Sir Edmund Godfrey didst fold and fashion, and then and there the said Sir Edmund Godfrey, feloniously, wilfully, and of thy malice aforethought didst choke and strangle, of which said choking and strangling the said Sir Edmund Godfrey instantly died."

Obviously the indictment was based only on Bedloe's evidence; there was no mention of Captain Atkins's affidavit. So much the better. Sam's alibis, supported by a host of witnesses, would clearly prove Mr. Bedloe mistaken about the man he had seen in Somerset House, the man who had called himself "Mr. Atkins, Pepys' clerk." Now Sam longed for his trial. The "day or two" suggested by Mr. Hayes on November 19 had long passed, and there was still no prospect of a trial. Of course (Sam told himself) the courts were very busy; one must have patience. But, "How long, Lord? Wilt thou be angry forever?"

The courts and the King's prosecutors were busy indeed. They had to deal not only with the usual run of malefactors but also with men accused of high treason, usually in connection with the Popish Plot. However, any Catholic was fair game for venal informers.

On November 21, as a curtain raiser to the Popish Plot trials, a Catholic goldsmith, Mr. William Staley, was tried for high treason at the Court of the King's Bench in Westminster Hall. Two unsavory informers named Carstairs and Sutherland swore that in a cook's shop, the Black Lion in King Street, they had heard Staley declare, in French, "The King of England is the greatest heretic and the greatest rogue in the world. Here is the heart and here is the hand that would kill him, I myself." Since even to imagine killing the King was construed as high treason, Staley, if convicted, would die horribly.

The two rogues had tried to blackmail Staley. When he refused to pay, they informed against him, perhaps to warn future blackmail victims that they meant business. Dr. Gilbert Burnet, Chaplain of the Rolls, who knew the informers to be professional liars, protested that no one should be tried on the word of such profligate wretches. But Lord Shaftesbury said, "We must support the evidence, and all those who undermine the credit of the witnesses are to be looked upon as public enemies." No one asked if the informers understood French.

Staley could hardly hope for a fair trial in maddened London. Moreover, the presiding judge, brawny, broad-faced Sir William Scroggs, Lord Chief Justice, was violent, intemperate, a fanatical believer in the Plot, and a bigoted anti-Catholic. Staley's trial was brief. The Frenchman to whom he had been talking was charged with the same offense (but never tried), and therefore could not testify in his friend's behalf. Staley denied that he had said the words quoted, but he could produce no evidence to support his denial, and, of course, he was a Papist. He admitted the fact and said that he hoped to live and die a Roman Catholic.

The jury pronounced him guilty, and Lord Chief Justice Scroggs said, with grim pleasantry, "Now you may die a Roman Catholic, and when you come to die I don't doubt you will be found a priest too." Then he pronounced the sentence for high treason according to form: "That you, the prisoner at the bar, be conveyed hence to the place from whence you came [Newgate], and from thence that you be drawn to the place of execution upon a hurdle, that there you be hanged by the neck, that you be cut down alive, that your privy members be cut off and your bowels taken out and burnt in your view, that your head be severed from your body, that your body be divided into quarters and those quarters be disposed at the King's pleasure—and the God of infinite mercy be merciful to your soul." On November 26, the butchery was performed at Tyburn before a screaming mob of exultant Protestants.

On November 27, Mr. Edward Coleman, the Duchess of York's secretary, was tried for high treason in proposing a rebellion that could result in the King's death and in trying to get assistance ("armed help," the lawyers called it) from France. Because this was the first public appearance of the great "Doctor" Oates in all the glory of his silk gown, cassock, scarf, and shovel hat, Westminster Hall was filled to the window sills. Lord Chief Justice Scroggs was very respectful to the savior of the nation, addressing him always as "Doctor," a title to which he had no shadow of right. There was unintentional irony in Scroggs's remark to Oates, "You have taken an oath, and you being a minister know the great regard you ought to have to the sacredness of an oath, and that to take a man's life away by a false oath is murder. I need not teach you that."

Thus admonished, Oates proceeded to lie his head off. He repeated with unction much of what he had formerly deposed about Coleman and the Plot, weaving a sticky web about the prisoner. Captain Bedloe, now Oates's principal aide, confirmed his chief's evidence, adding a few lurid lies of his own. Coleman denied all the informers' charges and put up a stout defense, but his foolish letters (five of which were read to the jury), the prosecution lawyers, and the madness of the times were all too much for him. The jury was told at last, "You must find the prisoner guilty or bring in two persons perjured." Faced with such a choice, the jury took only a few minutes to find the prisoner guilty. Like Staley, Coleman was condemned to be hanged, drawn, and quartered. The sentence was carried out on December 3, with Coleman protesting his innocence to the last.

The news of the two trials filtered into Newgate, and every Catholic prisoner gave himself up to despair. The prisoners always knew when there was to be a hanging. At dawn on execution day, the great bell of St. Sepulchre's would begin to toll, and a crowd would gather in the street before the prison gate. The muttering rumble of voices would rise to a roar as the victim was brought out, bound hand and foot, and placed on a hurdle or a cart, according to his sentence—a cart for a simple hanging. Then, as the procession rolled up Snow Hill on its way to Tyburn, the mob pelting the prisoner with anything at hand, the tumult and shouting would slowly die away and the bell would toll alone. Sam Atkins, cursed with imagination, found himself trembling, as if the waves of mob hatred had penetrated the stone walls to his cell. It was hard to concentrate on his thoughts or his Bible.

Mr. Pepys was having his troubles and anxieties too. The Opposition leaders wanted his head, and his inveterate enemy among them, Mr. William Harbord, wanted his job for himself. Mr. Pepys had earlier sent his Catholic musician, Morelli, to safety out of London, and he made sure that all his other servants were staunch Protestants. He had to be sure, also, that there were no Catholics in the Navy; he had to go warily about his daily affairs, prepared for a surprise attack.

On November 28, in the House of Commons, the Speaker informed the members of a charge that Mr. Pepys had granted passes to some Jesuits to go beyond seas. Mr. Pepys rose to answer.

"I am much more beholden to you, Mr. Speaker," he said with mild irony, "than to the member that informed you. I challenge any man that can say I ever conversed with a Jesuit, spoke with, or granted him a pass, in my life."

"One Dr. Conquest got a pass by means of Mr. Atkins—" Mr. Thomas Bennet, a young protégé of Lord Shaftesbury, paused significantly "—Pepys' clerk, for Mr. Thimbleby, a Jesuit, to go beyond seas."

"As for Thimbleby," said Mr. Pepys, "I never granted him a pass, and he never asked me for a pass, and granting of passes is wholly foreign to my employment."

Colonel Birch threw out a feeler. "Pepys says 'that he never conversed with a Jesuit nor granted him a pass,' and so forth. It lies on the other side to prove it. Atkins is said to be a servant of Pepys. I believe he can give you an account where Atkins was Saturday, Sunday, and Monday, when Godfrey was missing,"

How much did Colonel Birch know? Certainly he would learn nothing from Mr. Pepys, who said with dignified innocence, "Atkins was servant to my head clerk, and one year out of his apprenticeship. Where he was Saturday, Sunday, and Monday I know not, for I was those three days with the King at Newmarket. If you ask me of his deportment, I can bring those of my family who will be ready to tell you."

Of course, the Secretary was not strictly truthful, but he had no intention of showing his hand until all the cards were dealt. He had to play a waiting game. At the moment he thought he had all he needed to defeat his and Sam Atkins's enemies, but he was disturbed by the drift of affairs. The new Test Act was about to be approved, and twenty-one peers would lose their seats in the House of Lords—not, God be thanked, the Duke of York, who would be excepted by a special proviso. There was even talk that the King would recognize the Duke of Monmouth as his legitimate heir! What would the madness of fear and faction bring next?

On December 5, Mr. Pepys wrote to his sister, Paulina Jackson, at Brampton, Huntingdonshire, assuring her of his health and peace of mind. "One misfortune there is indeed," he wrote, "which has created me much trouble, namely that by a most manifest contrivance one of my clerks (Atkins) has been accused and is now in custody as a party some way concerned in the death of Sir Edmund Bury Godfrey; which (though most untrue) cannot be thought to pass in the world at so jealous a time as this without some reflections upon me as his master, and on that score does occasion me not a little disquiet. But I thank God I have not only my own innocence to satisfy myself with, but such an assurance of his also as that I make no question of his being able to acquit himself with advantage to him and infamy to his accusers; and that being done, the care which this accident occasions me will soon be over." This was all very reassuring to a sister, but Mr. Pepys was by no means sure. What if Sam Atkins should break and, to save his own life, confess to a crime he never committed?

Through Captain Richardson the Secret Committee of lords had kept a close watch on Sam Atkins. The Keeper waited until Sam had written himself out; then—illegally, of course—he siezed all his papers and carried them to the Committee. When the lords learned that Sam had an alibi for the time of Godfrey's murder, they were furious.

Refusing to believe Sam's account, the Committee summoned Captain Vittles and the sailors from the *Katherine* to appear for questioning on December 13.

On the appointed day, Mr. Michael Godfrey (one of Sir Edmund's younger brothers) appeared first before the Committee to complain that Sam Atkins was a prisoner at large and not in chains. Then Captain Bedloe, always ready with a brave new lie, came in to assert with an air of injured innocence that Sam's sister and "two great fellows" had come to his chamber door and had threatened him with what they would do to him if Sam should hang. He complained, too, that he was kept very short of money. The lords shook their heads sadly, commiserated with the captain, and promised protection and money. At last (but with Captain Bedloe and the Attorney General, Sir William Jones, in the room), the lords summoned Captain Vittles and his men.

Captain Vittles, a bluff, outspoken tar, deposed that he commanded the yacht *Katherine* until October 18. On October 14, Mr. Samuel Atkins and the Williams sisters came aboard the yacht at Greenwich about half past four in the afternoon and stayed aboard until about half past ten at night. Captain Vittles sent them back up-river in the four-oared wherry belonging to the yacht. Because the tide was strongly against it, the wherry went no farther than Billingsgate, below London Bridge, where the passengers disembarked and took a hackney coach in Thames Street. The boat returned to the yacht just at midnight.

Corroborating statements were made by boatswain William Tribbett and common seamen George Stephenson and William French. Richard Dickson said that he took ashore a Holland cheese and six bottles of wine (gifts from Captain Vittles), which he put in the coach with Sam Atkins, who was "much in drink," and had slept most of the way up-river.

Fortunately the sailors were all Protestants. Catholics were supposed to have dispensations permitting them to lie without incurring the wrath of God. The lords bullied the sailors unmercifully, trying to shake their stories or to catch them in contradictions, but there was no doubt about it: Sam Atkins had a cast-iron alibi for the night of October 14.

At this point, in simple decency, Lord Shaftesbury and his crew should have ordered Sam released at once. However, a grand jury had already indicted him. To file a *nolle prosequi* would cause a deal of talk and cast doubt upon Captain Bedloe's authority as a witness. Because two concurring witnesses were needed in trials for high treason, the faction had to have both Oates and Bedloe to convict those charged with complicity in the Popish Plot. Moreover the Opposition leaders dared not admit a mistake. To that many-headed monster, the London mob, they had to appear infallible, wiser and stronger than the King himself.

Anyway, there was still Captain Charles Atkins's affidavit charging Sam as accessory to Godfrey's murder. The captain's story was so amateurish and unconvincing that the faction feared what might happen in a legal duel, especially with the redoubtable Secretary Pepys as Sam's second. Given time and the pestilential breath of Newgate, Sam Atkins might yet break and confess, thereby implicating Mr. Pepys.

The leaders of the faction spaced their trials and executions with care, producing one or the other whenever the national madness showed signs of moderating. On December 17, Fathers Thomas Whitebread, John Fenwick, and William Ireland were tried for high treason at the Old Bailey, along with Thomas Pickering, a Benedictine lay brother, and John Grove, a Catholic layman. In his *Narrative* Oates had accused Pickering and Grove of trying to assassinate the King.

The Old Bailey, across the street from Newgate, was packed to the rafters with spectators who had come as much to see Titus Oates in all his splendor as to watch the trial. The bandy-legged hero gave damning false evidence against all five prisoners. Bedloe, perhaps made cautious by the Atkins debacle, trimmed his sails and would only say that he had heard Ireland, Pickering, and Grove discussing plans for a new assassination attempt. With only one witness against them, Whitebread and Fenwick should have been freed; instead, against law and usage, they were sent back to Newgate to wait until Captain Bedloe found a fair wind again.

Lord Chief Justice Scroggs summed up the evidence against Ireland, Pickering, and Grove in a masterly denunciation of Catholics, accusing them of debauching men's understandings, overturning all morals, and destroying all divinity. "Nay," he concluded, "when they have licenses to sin and indulgences for falsehoods—when they can make him a saint that dies in one and then pray to him, as the carpenter first makes an image and afterwards worships it—and can then think to bring that wooden religion of theirs among us in this nation, what shall I think of them? . . . They eat their God, they kill their king, and they saint the murderer. They indulge in all sorts of sins and no human bonds can hold them!" The three men were convicted, of course. Hoping for a lucid break in the clouds of insanity, King Charles postponed their executions as long as he dared, to the annoyance of Lord Shaftesbury and the fury of the mob.

On December 21, the spotlight flickered back to the murder of Sir Edmund Bury Godfrey. Miles Prance, a goldsmith and a former Catholic, was informed against by his lodger, John Wren, who owed him fourteen months' rent. The charge was that Prance, a friend of various imprisoned Jesuits, had been absent from his house in Princes Street, Covent Garden, for two or three nights during the week of October 6-14, "about the time of Sir Edmund Godfrey's disappearance." Prance, an intelligent man but rather weak and timid, was arrested and brought to the lobby of the House of Commons to be examined.

While he was waiting (so the story goes), Captain Bedloe entered the lobby and learned who the prisoner was and the charges against him. When he heard that the goldsmith had no alibi for the time of Godfrey's murder,

Bedloe saw his chance. An hour or so later the guards took Prance to a nearby cook shop, an "ordinary" called cheerfully "Heaven," in which Bedloe was purposely planted. When Prance came in, Bedloe started up and cried, "This is one of the rogues I saw with a dark lantern about the body of Sir Edmund Bury Godfrey, but he was then in a periwig!"

Of course Bedloe's recognition was a cheat, a flam. Out of favor because of his timidity at the trial of Whitebread and Fenwick, he had to do something to reestablish his reputation as an informer and to provide the faction with a scapegoat for Godfrey's murder. To the experienced sharper, Prance, a thin, bent man with fair hair and a short beard, had all the look of a light-timbered fellow who could be led by the nose. Bedloe's estimate was correct.

Severely examined by a committee of the Commons, Prance stoutly protested his innocence. A day and a night in irons in the bitter cold of Newgate's condemned hole broke him. Late on December 22, he asked to be taken to see Lord Shaftesbury at his mansion on Aldersgate Street, in the City. The next morning he was examined in Newgate by the Secret Committee of lords. On the day before Christmas, to the King and the Privy Council, Prance confessed his complicity in Godfrey's murder and accused five others: two Irish priests, Gerard and Kelly, and three laymen, Robert Green, the elderly cushion keeper of the Queen's chapel in Somerset House, Lawrence Hill, servant to Dr. Godden, treasurer of the chapel, and Henry Berry, a porter at Somerset House. The first two laymen were avowed Catholics. Berry, who had changed his religion to keep his job, promptly declared himself a Protestant again.

Godfrey was murdered, said Prance, because he was a bitter persecutor" of Catholics and "a particular enemy of the Queen's servants." Prance was an unwilling accomplice and a witness to the murder. On the night of Saturday, October 12, as Godfrey walked along the Strand past Somerset House, Berry and Kelly pretended to be quarreling in the courtyard of the palace. Hill intercepted the justice, and begged him to intervene lest blood be shed. As Godfrey walked toward the two quarreling men, Green throttled him from behind with a large, twisted handkerchief; the four others leaped upon him, beat him and kicked him, and Green wrung his neck.

The murderers (said Prance) kept Godfrey's body in a room in Somerset House. On Monday, November 14, they moved it to another room, and that night all of them gathered to inspect it by the light of a dark lantern. At midnight on Wednesday, October 16, they set the corpse on horseback and took it to a ditch near Primrose Hill, thrusting the magistrate's own sword through his body to give the appearance of suicide.

This, in brief, was Prance's confession. One can hardly help seeing Lord Shaftesbury's hand in it. If he did not tell Prance what to say, he surely told him what not to say. There is no reason to suspect that Prance knew what Bedloe had earlier testified about the murder. Certainly he could not know that all but one of the men named by Bedloe had disappeared, and that the one, Sam Atkins, had a perfect alibi. We can almost hear Lord Shaftesbury wheedling, coaxing, and finally threatening, "Nay, Mr. Prance, you were there that night; Captain Bedloe has sworn positively against you. Now who were the others? I'll tell you what, you have a simple choice. Confess and you shall have a full pardon. Refuse and you'll be hanged."

Prance wanted to live. Like every other Londoner he knew from the evidence given at the inquest how Godfrey had died and that two or more men had murdered him. It was the talk of the town that he had been killed in Somerset House, and Prance knew the building well. Perhaps, shivering with cold and fright, and desperately casting about for names, he picked on the two Irish priests, Gerard and Kelly, because he knew they were safely out of the country. "Any laymen? Come, Mr. Prance, be ingenuous with me." Lord Shaftesbury had his man pinned like a butterfly. Yes—and Prance named Green, Berry, and Hill, perhaps because they were associated with Somerset House and the first to come to mind. No one will ever know why. There is only one certainty: the three victims were innocent.

This time Shaftesbury could not suggest that Prance name Sam Atkins. Captain Bedloe had already queered his pitch by placing Prance with Godfrey's killers in Somerset House on the night of October 14, at the very time for which Sam Atkins had an alibi. No matter; Shaftesbury desperately needed live bodies for Jack Ketch and the bloodthirsty rabble, and Prance could deliver them. As for Sam Atkins, let him rot in jail; perhaps he could still be charged as an accessory. Conveniently enough, the alleged murderers (said Prance) had told him that "there should be one more in [the conspiracy] whose name he doth not remember." An accessory did not have to be on the scene of the crime.

Now London had a new sensation. Proclamations went out for Gerard and Kelly, who were never found, and messengers seized Green, Berry, and Hill and carried them to Newgate. Unfortunately, Prance, brooding in a reasonably temperate cell in Newgate, discovered that he had a conscience. On December 29, before the King and the Privy Council, he retracted his confession and swore that he knew nothing about the murder or the Plot. Back he went to Newgate for a longer period of treatment in a frigid underground cell. On January 10, Dr. William Lloyd visited him and found him half frozen and unable to speak. When Lloyd came again the next day, Prance, who had been thawed out and moved to a warmer cell, was able to repeat his original confession. That day he began to write, and under Caqtain Richardson's careful supervision he soon finished his *True Narrative and Discovery of . . . The Horrid Popish Plot.* On January 14, Prance was pardoned and soon after released from prison.

There is an ugly story about a conversation some time later between one Mr. William Smith and Oates, Bedloe, and Prance. Said Mr. Smith, "Coming one evening to visit [Oates] at Whitehall, I found Bedloe and Prance with him; amongst other discourses they talked of Sir Edmund Bury Godfrey. Oates laughed at the business and said, 'Here is Bedloe, that knew no more of the business than you or I did. But he got the £500, and that did his work, and he gave this blockhead £30 of it. He picked him up in the lobby of the House [of Commons] and took him for a loggerhead fit for his purpose.' At which Bedloe laughed heartily, and Prance seemed a little dull and displeased."

Meanwhile, ignorant of his fate, Sam Atkins dragged out the days in Newgate. Even Christmas and Twelfth Night, with all their festivities, brought little joy to the melancholy inmates. In the great room of the Felons' Common side, there was a sea-coal fire on Christmas Day and plenty of boiled beef for once, but no plum porridge or Christmas pies, nothing to relieve the wintry gloom. At least Sam was now a prisoner "at large," and he was not in chains. Within certain limits he was free to roam through the dark corridors and filthy common rooms of the jail.

To a law-abiding young man who had never before seen the inside of a prison, Newgate—"the King's Head Inn," as the canting crew called it—must have been a horrible revelation. He would be sure to pass by "Jack Ketch's Kitchen," where the heads and reeking quarters of executed traitors lay in baskets until the hangman parboiled them with bay salt and aromatic cummin seed before spiking them on the walls and gates of London. He would rub elbows with all sorts and conditions of prisoners, most of them in shackles, from broken tradesmen imprisoned for debt and Quakers imprisoned for their religion, to sneaking "bung-nippers," who would try to pick his pockets, and "knights of the road" or "rum padders" —swaggering highwaymen, the aristocrats of Newgate. Here would be a cluster of beggars in a common-room, huddled together for warmth like a pile of old rags, sleeping on the bare floor beside the buckets of night soil; there a pair of sharpers engaged in "putting the doctor" on a gull—cheating him with false dice. Here would be a qualmish drunkard easing his stomach; there a noisy gang of roisterers, men and half-naked women, heated and fuddled by Nantes brandy; nearby a fanatic praying on his knees, a sick man tended by a compassionate friend, and a penitent thief reading *The Whole Duty of Man,* a famous moral homily.

There was no segregation of the sexes. Common whores, "punks," "drabs," and "bulkers," were sent to Bridewell to beat hemp, but there was no lack of "buttocks," "trulls," and "doxies" committed to Newgate for theft or debt. Some of them, spying a spruce young fellow, would try to woo him to bed, partly for pleasure, partly in hopes of becoming pregnant and getting a stay of execution by pleading "a great belly."

But Sam Atkins tells us nothing about any adventures in Newgate. Perhaps familiarity and custom reconciled him to his fate and made hell tolerable. We can be sure that he attended services every Sunday in the dingy chapel on the topmost floor of the prison. We know that he was now allowed visitors, including the learned and pious Dr. John Tillotson, Dean of Canterbury, who came twice or thrice at Sam's request and brought the prisoner diversion and spiritual comfort. From various friends who came to see him, Sam could have learned something of what was going on in the outside world: how thirty thousand Papists and suspected Papists had been driven from their homes in London; how Titus Oates had publicly accused Queen Catherine of conspiring with her physician, Sir George Wakeman, to poison the King; how Parliament had insisted on disbanding the royal forces in Flanders; how there had been a strange alarm of one thousand French troops landing in the Isle of Purbeck; how another informer, Stephen Dugdale, had come out of Staffordshire with exciting new information about the Popish Plot; and how the House of Commons had impeached Lord Treasurer Danby for high treason.

But these were matters above Sam's sphere and of only passing interest. Much more important to him were some items about Captain Charles Atkins, that rogue in grain, who had publicly declared his malice against Secretary Pepys, had sworn that he would find out much to do him an unkindness, and had bragged that the King was pleased with his services as an informer. He fully expected to be pardoned for his past misdeeds and to be given command of a frigate bound for Barbadoes.

It seems, too, that late in November, when Mr. John Powell, a London merchant, was unaccountably missing from his home and a reward of £200 was posted for news of him, Captain Charles had boasted that he knew where Powell was, that Sam Atkins had told him that Powell had been sent to Rouen in France—probably by Mr. Pepys. ("You did not tell me neither that your master had a house in Rouen, in France, did you?"). Two days later Powell turned up at Worcester, alive and well, and Captain Atkins's cake was dough.

What Sam's friends did not know was that on January 1, 1679, the former naval captain Charles Atkins was commissoned as lieutenant to Captain Charles Lawson in Sir John Fenwick's Regiment of Foot. Now, as a King's officer again, he had status and respectability, and his value as a witness was enhanced. His commission was, in effect, a full pardon for his past misdeeds.

Early in January came a great day for Sam Atkins: he learned about Prance's confession, and that Prance had said in answer to a question that "he knows not Atkins." For the first time in many weeks Sam had some faint hopes of life and freedom. With Prance's confession and his own alibi for October 14, he no longer feared Captain Bedloe's testimony. Now, unless his enemies had some legal trick in prospect, or a new informer in reserve, Sam's trial would become a duel between the prisoner and Captain Charles.

Sam fought desperately for a trial. Not only would he have a chance to prove his innocence before all the world, but he could pour out his stored-up wrath against Charles

Atkins. He pictured himself in court overwhelming the perfidious wretch with facts, logic, and solemn appeals to Almighty God. Perhaps he could force Charles to eat his words, to admit in open court that he had lied. But Sam could not get his trial. Michaelmas Term had ended on November 28; Hilary Term ran from January 23, 1679, to February 12. The days crept by in slow, agonizing procession, and still Sam's counsel could not get his client's name on the crowded docket.

On January 24, 1679, the day on which King Charles reluctantly dissolved the Long Parliament and called for new elections, Ireland and Grove were at last butchered at Tyburn. Pickering was reprieved again until May 9. The Popish Plot terror was at its height.

It was a cold winter with hard frosts and some snow. The sun rarely shone, and the nights were ages long. In Newgate everybody suffered.

On February 2, 1679, a Westminster grand jury indicted Green, Berry, and Hill for the murder of Sir Edmund Bury Godfrey. Well instructed by the leaders of the faction, the jury next indicted Samuel Atkins as an accessory. The indictment charged that Sam did "command, counsel, and abet" Green, Berry, and Hill, and that after the murder he did "harbor, comfort, and maintain" the murderers "against the peace of our sovereign lord the King, his crown and dignity." Now there were two indictments against Sam Atkins. His counsel had recourse to a writ of *habeas corpus.* Since the prosecutors were now ready for Sam, the writ was accepted, and on Saturday, February 8, two keepers conducted the prisoner from Newgate to the Court of the King's Bench to be arraigned.

As usual Westminster Hall was crowded. The booths of booksellers, toy sellers, and seamstresses along the walls were busy; the Court of Common Pleas against the right-hand wall was packed with brawling lawyers and litigants; and at the upper end of the great hall the Courts of King's Bench and Chancery were in full session. The keepers pushed through the crowds until they were close enough to catch the court clerk's eye.

When the current case was finished and the verdict brought in, the three robed and bewigged judges on their high bench settled back, and Chief Justice Scroggs nodded to the court clerk, who summoned Samuel Atkins. In the majestic presence of the law, Sam felt like a truant school-boy.

"Samuel Atkins, hold up thy hand," said the court clerk. Sam held up his right hand while the clerk read the grand jury's indictment in tedious detail, concluding, "How sayest thou, Samuel Atkins, art thou guilty as accessory to the said felony and murder whereof thou standest indicted and hast now been arraigned, or not guilty?"

"Not guilty," said Sam in a quavering voice.

"Culprit, how wilt thou be tried?"

Prompted by a keeper, Sam replied, according to form, "By God and my country."

"God send thee a good deliverance," said the court clerk, also according to form.

Sam appealed to the Lord Chief Justice, "My lord, I do humbly desire that the several examinations taken concerning this business may at my trial be brought into court."

"Why, Mr. Atkins," said Scroggs, "do you know nothing of this business that you are so willing to have all the evidence brought in against you?"

"My lord, I know nothing of it at all."

"Are you a Papist, Mr. Atkins?"

"No, my lord, I am not."

"Were you ever one?"

"No, I never was one, not I hope never shall be. When is it that your lordship pleases to have me tried, for I have lain these sixteen weeks in prison and do earnestly desire my trial."

Scroggs looked at the troublesome young fellow with some annoyance; he was going to be a problem. "You shall be tried as soon as we can. We must try the others on Monday, and if there be time afterwards you may be tried then. However, Captain Richardson shall have a rule to bring you up then." With this promise Sam had to be content.

On Monday, February 10, half of London flocked to

Westminster Hall for the trials of Green, Berry, and Hill. When Captain Richardson arrived with Sam and his many witnesses, the vast hall was so packed that some of the crowd had overflowed into the jury box and had to be forcibly removed. The Court of the King's Bench and the Court of Chancery were on steps well above floor level, but what with the dark of a cloudy day and the smoke and fog drifting in through the open windows, the courts were almost hidden from view. Sam and his friends could make out the white wigs and scarlet robes of the three King's Bench judges on their elevated bench, and they had glimpses of the King's witnesses, Oates, Bedloe, and Prance. They could not hear the despairing attempts of the three culprits to prove their innocence, but at the end of the trial, when the jury returned, they knew by the crowd's approving roar that in each case the verdict was "Guilty."

Sam Atkins was not outraged by the verdict. Forced to face reality, he was losing some of his anti-Catholic hatred, but, like everybody else, he believed that there had been a Popish Plot and that Sir Edmund Godfrey had been murdered by fiendish Papists. Mr. Prance had confessed his part in the murder, God be thanked! The King had pardoned him; therefore, he must be telling the truth.

But Sam pitied the three condemned men; he could feel for them. All too often of late he had had a vivid dream of standing on a cart with Jack Ketch at Tyburn, his hands bound behind him, a rope around his neck, and thousands of savage eyes glaring at him, thousands of savage voices screaming hate. The cart pulled away. He fell with a jerk —not enough to break his neck—and kicked, twisted, and strangled, while his friends—he hoped he would have friends to do him one last kindness—pulled on his legs to shorten his struggles. He always awakened from such dreams bathed in a cold sweat.

Seventeenth-century law was swift; at three o'clock in the afternoon the show was over. The mob streamed out through the front doors into New Palace Yard, and Sam Atkins and his party fought their way to the bar of the court. Lord Chief Justice Scroggs, tired but triumphant, scowled at Sam. Sir William Jones, the bullying Attorney-General, and a prominent member of the Opposition party, had been present when the Secret Committee of lords examined Captain Vittles and his men. He knew that Sam Atkins had an alibi for October 14, and it would be strange indeed if Scroggs did not know it too, as well as what the King's prosecutors had in mind. However, it was nearly the end of the term, and Scroggs was tired.

"Mr. Atkins," he said, "have you any bail ready?"

Bail? Sam was dismayed. To live for months with an indictment hanging over his head! Even more than his freedom, Sam passionately wanted vindication.

"No, my lord," he said. "I am prepared for my trial, if your lordship pleases, but not with bail."

"Aye, but, Mr. Atkins, it is the latter end of the term, and many people's livelihoods lie at stake. We cannot lay aside all business for yours."

"My lord," Sam pleaded, "my life lies at stake, and I have been under severe imprisonment a long time. I humbly pray I may be tried. Besides, I have many witnesses, who have remained in town on purpose to give evidence for me ever since the last term. I hope my trial will not take up much time."

"If you have so many witnesses," said Justice Dolben, "it cannot be soon over."

"I have many ready," Sam countered, "but I hope I shall have occasion to use only a few."

"Mr. Atkins, we cannot do it," said Scroggs. "You must be content. You shall be tried at the sessions, but in the meantime you shall be bailed."

"I submit, my lord. I think I have bail here." Somewhere in the cluster of Sam's friends was the squat form of Secretary Pepys, come to witness the trial. Surely he would go bail for a repentant sinner; he was noted for compassion.

But Captain David Lloyd, a gentleman-captain who looked upon lawyers and judges with contempt, spoke up sharply. "My lord, I am a witness on behalf of this gentleman, and cannot possibly be in England a fort-night hence."

"My lord," said Sam, "this is a captain of one of the King's ships, and his occasions will indispensably call him away, and this is the case of several others of my witnesses."

Scroggs was disturbed. A captain of one of the King's ships! Present by the King's command, no doubt. Scroggs was a time-server, slavishly following the line of power. Now the Opposition grandees were in power, but the King was still the King, God's anointed. Like all bullies, Scroggs cringed before authority.

"Well, I do not know," he said. "If it be so, you shall be tried tomorrow." He turned to Captain Rich-ardson. "And so bring him up very early."

Early on Tuesday, February 11, at the Court of the King's Bench, Green, Berry, and Hill stood in chains to hear little Justice Wild sermonize on the odious sin of murder. He concluded with their sentence: "That you go from hence to the place from whence you came, and from thence to the place of execution, where you shall be severally hanged by the neck until you are dead. And may God have mercy on your souls."

Robert Green, an elderly carpenter who, according to Prance, had strangled Godfrey with a handkerchief and had afterwards broken the magistrate's neck, found his voice. "God save the King!" he cried. "And I desire all good people to pray for us." Jack Ketch tied each victim's thumbs together with whipcord, and bailiffs led the three away, clanking in their chains.

Sam Atkins and his "cloud of reputable witnesses" took their place at the bar below the three judges, Chief Justice Scroggs, Justice Sir William Wild, and Justice Sir William Dolben. As a special favor, Sam was not fettered. At his right was the jury box, soon to be filled with twelve good men and true. In front of the box was a bench for the King's prosecutors: Sir William

Jones, the Attorney-General ("bullfaced Jonas" the poet Dryden called him); eloquent Sir Francis Winnington, the Solicitor General; sharp-tongued Sir George Jeffreys, Recorder of London; and Sergeant Sir Thomas Stringer— a formidable array of legal talent.

At the sight of their grim faces, Sam Atkins lost heart for a moment. Behind him were his friends, his fellow clerks, Captain Lloyd, Captain Vittles and his men, Mrs. Bulstrode and her maid, Mr. Hewer, and many more. Somewhere in the little crowd below was Secretary Pepys, incognito; but Sam Atkins had to face the prosecutors alone, with no one allowed to prompt him or whisper advice. Sam was understandably tense and nervous, but he put his trust in God, his own wits, and the testimony of his friends.

After the Crown Clerk had prosed through the indictments, the jurors—twelve respectable Middlesex gentlemen—were chosen, sworn in, and seated. Time was wasted in discussing the problem of the two conflicting indictments. The prosecution could not simply drop the first indictment against Sam as the principal in Godfrey's murder; it had to be read aloud, and the jury had to be instructed to find him not guilty of that charge. He was to be tried as an accessory to the murder.

Opening for the prosecution, Sergeant Stringer spent most of his time clearing up the confusion about the two indictments. Following him, Sir William Jones went over the same ground, adding gratuitously that "I must say this much to Mr. Atkins, that he hath cause to bless God that ever Mr. Prance made this discovery, for I assure you, without that, there are those circumstances, probabilities, and presumptions that he might have gone in grave danger of being accounted a principal in the murder." Jones was adept at turning presumptions into damning conclusions. His manner was politely malevolent.

Sam very well knew how much he owed to Mr. Prance. In fact, he was then in court, ready to testify that he knew nothing about Sam, had never heard of him, and had never before seen his face.

Continuing, Sir William Jones told the jury what Mr. Charles Atkins would say, confusing the Lord Chief Justice by the identity of surnames. "Charles Atkins," said Jones patiently, "is the witness. Samuel Atkins is the prisoner. It was Samuel that complained to Charles of Sir Edmund Bury Godfrey, enquiring after the courage and resolution of Child, and ordered Charles to send him thither."

Next Jones told the jury what Captain Bedloe would say, that he had seen Samuel Atkins standing by Godfrey's body in Somerset House. "For we have this proof against him. Bedloe finding a young man there whom he did not know, he went up to him, desiring to know his name. He tells him who he was, one Atkins, and describes himself by a particular circumstance to whom he had relation, and Mr. Bedloe will tell you though the light was not very great, yet it was enough to let him see the faces of those he took notice of, and that this prisoner was there, and if this be true, it will have the effect of proving him guilty as accessory, either before or after the fact." Sir William Jones was a ruthless prosecutor, who sought convictions even at the price of truth.

Mr. Charles Atkins came forward. We may take it that Charles—no longer Captain Atkins—was not wearing the buff coat and red breeches of a sailor. Now he was an army officer and a courtier, in a fine coat, a flowered waistcoat, a blonde periwig and beaver hat, with lace at throat and wrists and a light dress sword at his side.

Charles repeated at length the story he had told so many times before, his shabby fiction about Sam Atkins, John Child, and Mr. Pepys of the Navy. Scroggs followed the account closely, now and then asking Charles to repeat what he had just said. The fact that the noisy Court of Chancery was separated from the King's bench only by a thin board partition made hearing difficult. When Charles had finished, Scroggs summed up his testimony neatly: "Then all Samuel Atkins said to you was that Sir Edmund Bury Godfrey had much injured his master, and if he lived would ruin him; and then asked you if you knew a man that would be stout and secret, and bid you send him to his master, but not ask for him."

By removing Sam Atkins's supposed words from the context of Charles's full account, Scroggs made them seem harmless and empty. Observers must have wondered what had come over the Lord Chief Justice. Always before, in the Popish Plot trials, Scroggs had made much of the evidence given by the King's witnesses, emphasizing those items most damaging to the victims. Now he was completely reversing his usual practice.

Almost bursting with eagerness to prove Charles Atkins a liar, Sam was allowed only a few trifling questions about dates and places. Then Attorney-General Jones, a lawyer with an undeserved reputation for honesty, introduced a surprise witness, saying, "Now, my lord, because it seems a strange thing that Mr. Atkins, who says he is a Protestant, should be engaged in this business, we have a witness here to prove that he hath been seen often at Somerset House at Mass, and so he is a party concerned; for those that are of the Catholic party, it was their interest to cut Sir Edmund Bury Godfrey off. And the witness is this boy, an angel from Heaven to deliver the truth."

Then entered "a little boy, by his habit supposed to be one of the black guard"—a set of young rogues who loitered about the Horse Guards' barracks near Whitehall and made a thin living wiping shoes, cleaning boots, watering horses, running errands, and carrying torches for pedestrians at night. Before the boy could be sworn, quick-witted Sam Atkins, who stood at one side with his crowd of witnesses and with nothing to mark him as the prisoner, smelled a rat and spoke up.

"What religion are you of, boy?" he asked.

"A Protestant."

"Do you know me?"

"No."

"Sir," said Justice Wild to Sam angrily, "you are too bold with the witness."

Taken aback by Sam's readiness, the prosecution lawyers could only make excuses, plead a mistake ("I have him not in my brief," said Jones), and sent the boy away, with a scolding to the prosecutor's clerk who had brought him in. Had the prisoner been brought to the bar and identified, the "angel from Heaven" would have sworn that Sam Atkins was a Papist, and the jury might well have condemned him out of hand.

The prosecution called Captain Bedloe. Dressed in the height of Court fashion, the informer made a great impression on the jury; unfortunately, aware of Sam's alibi, Bedloe would swear to nothing.

"Your lordship," he said, "had an account yesterday how Le Faire came to acquaint me that such an one was murdered and that they intended so and so to dispose of the body. When I came to meet him at Somerset House, I asked him who were to be concerned in carrying him off. He told me it was a gentleman, one Mr. Atkins. I thought it might have been this gentleman"—pointing to Charles Atkins—"whom I had known several years since, and so I enquired no further, but remembered he told me so; and when I came into the room, there were a great many there, and some of their faces I did see. I asked a young gentleman whether his name was not Atkins, and he said 'Yes;' then I asked him if he were Mr. Pepys' clerk. He answered 'Yes,' and added 'I have seen you often at my master's house.' There was a very little light, and the man was one I was not acquainted with, though I had been often at the house, but could never meet with him, and yet the man said he had seen me often there. So that it is hard for me to swear that this is he. I do not remember that he was such a person as the prisoner is; as far as I can remember he had a more manly face than he hath, and a beard."

No amount of prompting by the prosecution or the judges could get Bedloe to say more. He was careful to remind the court that he had not made a positive identification before the Secret Committee of lords.

"Indeed," said Sir William Jones, "he was never positive at the first." At all costs, Captain Bedloe's reputation as a King's witness must be kept untarnished. Unaware of the real reason for Bedloe's refusal to identify him, Sam Atkins was delighted. As far as he knew, Captain Bedloe was an honest man. Perhaps some day Bedloe would meet the imposter who had usurped Sam's name and identify him by his more manly face and beard.

The prosecution called one more witness, Mr. Thomas Walton, Sam's former schoolmaster at Hackney. The old gentleman, bright-eyed with importance and quite unaware that he might be doing Sam a disservice, came forward to swear that he had invited Sam to have dinner with him on October 12 at Mount Horeb, an ordinary in Pudding Lane. Sam had accepted the invitation, but had not come. Said the schoolmaster, "When I heard that this gentleman was in this unhappy affair, I said, how much better had it been for him to have been in my company, that I might have vouched for him."

Sam Atkins begged the court's leave to ask a question. He apologized to Mr. Walton for forgetting the appointment, and asked him to testify to his Protestantism.

"How was he bred, sir?" asked Scroggs.

"He was bred up in the Protestant religion, my lord."

"Were his father and mother Protestants?"

"Yes, my lord, they were so, and I knew them very well."

"Pray, sir," said Sam, "declare whether I was not only bred a Protestant, but whether I was not so also when I left your school."

"Yes, my lord," said Walton, "he was always a Protestant, and a very zealous one too."

"There is very much in that," said Scroggs, nodding wisely.

The prosecution had no more witnesses. Now Sam Atkins was called on to offer his defense. This was his moment of glory. Now, after weeks of humiliation, confinement, and misery, he could justify himself, prove his innocence to all the world, and put Charles Atkins to the shame he so richly deserved. Sam launched into a carefully memorized oration.

"My lord, and gentlemen of the jury, I hope I shall in my defense proceed very inoffensively towards God and towards this court. First, towards God (before whom I am, in whose presence I must appear, and before whom I can protest my innocence as to what is charged against me), in that I shall declare nothing but what is true. And towards this court in the next place, because I intend to deliver myself with all the respect and submission to it that becomes a prisoner.

"My lord, this gentleman, Mr. Atkins, who hath brought this accusation against me, is a man whom I have kept from perishing. I suppose he will own it himself. I petitioned, solicited for him, and was instrumental in getting him out of prison for a fact which I shall by and by tell you. And though this, my lord, may appear against me, yet by and by—"

"Hold!" said the Lord Chief Justice, "you mistake, Mr. Atkins, he does you no mischief at all. His account of his discourse with you is nothing to the purpose."

Cut short in full career, Sam was taken aback. "But I never had any such discourse with him, my lord," he protested.

"If you had or had not, it is no matter; you need not labor your defense as to anything he says."

Sam could hardly believe his ears. "I protest before God Almighty," he cried, "I know nothing of it!"

The Lord Chief Justice merely smiled and shook his head. Sam's very human dreams of heroism and revenge crashed in ruins. For a moment he was at a loss for words. Justice Dolben brought him back to reality.

"But what say you to Mr. Bedloe's testimony? Did you see the body of Sir Edmund Godfrey at Somerset House?"

"No, my lord. I am so far from that, that in all my life I was never in the house."

"Then call a couple of witnesses," said Scroggs, "to prove where you were that Monday night, the 14th of October, and you need not trouble yourself any further."

Suddenly Sam was aware that the atmosphere of the court had changed. The Lord Chief Justice was smiling—smiling!—and even the grim prosecution lawyers had relaxed. Sam was bewildered. Much later he realized that in a sense the whole trial had been staged, arranged so that the King's witnesses, Bedloe and Charles Atkins, (who might be useful some day), should come off with flying colors.

With Green, Berry, and Hill convicted of Godfrey's murder, there was no need for another victim. From force of habit, or sheer malice, the prosecution lawyers, knowing very well that Sam had an alibi for the night of October 14, had given him a hard time, even descending to such a rogue's trick as bringing in a suborned witness to prove him a Papist. Jones would have had no compunction about sending an innocent man to the gallows.

To Sam Atkins the rest of the trial was like a dream. Bluff Captain Vittles, who deposed that he had known Sam for fourteen years, provided his crucial alibi and some occasions for laughter. He told in laborious detail how he had come from Greenwich to Derby House for orders on the morning of October 14, and there had met Sam Atkins.

"I am glad you are not gone," Sam had said, "for there are a couple of gentlewomen that desire to see a yacht, and if you will go down I will come down too and bring my friends by and by."

"I am glad I am in a way to serve you," Captain Vittles had replied, "and you shall be welcome to what I have."

Disappointing some friends he had planned to meet at Billingsgate, Captain Vittles went back downstream to Greenwich and ordered his little ship swept and garnished and a collation prepared. At half past four Sam Atkins and the two "gentlewomen" (a word that covered a multitude of sinners) arrived by boat, inspected the yacht, admired its trim lines and polished brass-work, and joined the captain in his comfortable cabin for a glass or two of wine.

"—and the wine being good and just come from beyond seas, we drank till seven of the clock, and I would not let them go. Then said he, 'I will not keep the boat upon charge here.' 'No, you need not,' said I, 'my boat shall see you ashore.' So he discharged the boat, which was, I say, about seven o'clock, and so about eight or nine o'clock we had drunk till we were a little warm; and the wine drinking pretty fresh, and being with our friends, we did drink freely till it was indeed unseasonable. I must beg your lordship's pardon, but so it was. And at half an hour past ten I ordered my men to go off with the boat of four oars that belonged to the yacht that would go much swifter than any other boat, and I put him into the boat very much fuddled.

"Now, my lord, away goes he, with four of my men—they are here—and I ordered them, pray, said I, put ashore Mr. Atkins and his friends where they will go ashore. And because the tide was so strong at the bridge that they could not get through, they put them ashore at Billingsgate."

"Mr. Bedloe," said Scroggs, "what time of the night was it that you were at Somerset House?"

"It was between nine and ten," said Bedloe.

"He was on shipboard then," said Scroggs.

"He was very sober that you spoke withal," said Justice Wild to Bedloe. "Was he not?"

"Yes, very sober, my lord."

Scroggs turned to Captain Vittles again. "Then call for another witness," he said, "one of your men, and we have done."

"Give the word for the boatswain Tribbet," said the captain to the seamen grouped behind him.

Scroggs, who loved mightily a wench and a bottle, was pleased to be mildly facetious with the captain. "Did the women pledge you, captain?" he asked.

"Pledge me, my lord?" Vittles was not a gentleman-captain; he knew enough to drink to the health of his guests, but "pledge" was meaningless.

"Aye, did they drink with you?"

"Aye, and drink to us too, my lord."

Boatswain Tribbet confirmed the captain's testimony, and Scroggs was satisfied. So was the Attorney General, who threw in his hand, saying, "My lord, it is in vain to contend in a fact that is plain. But I would desire (because some perhaps will make an ill use of it) that they would please to take notice here is no disproving the King's evidence. For Mr. Bedloe did not at first, nor doth he now, charge him to be the man; so that whoever reports that the King's evidence is disproved will raise a very false rumor."

"No, no," said Scroggs, "It is so much otherwise that for all he hath said herein he is the more to be credited in his testimony; and Mr. Atkins needed not to make any defense, but must have come off without any upon what Mr. Bedloe says for him."

"So likewise for the first man," said Jones. "All that he says consists together and may be true, and yet Mr. Atkins innocent."

"So it may."

"I desire the company may not go away with a mistake, as if the King's evidence were disproved."

"Not a tittle," said Scroggs airily.

"Then I have done, my lord."

"No," said the Lord Chief Justice, "I will tell you how it did arise. It arose from the jealousy of the murder of Sir Edmund Godfrey, and persons were willing to lay hold on any opportunity to find it out. And Mr. Bedloe was told such a man should be his fellow to help him carry away the body; and hearing of such a name, thought it possible it might be such a one; and he owning himself to bear that name and to be Mr. Pepys' clerk, when Bedloe gave in his information, the people, who were put into such alarms as these, were very ready to catch at it. Therefore nobody was to blame for pursuing Bedloe's evidence. He said nothing then but what he says now, and that is nothing at all positive, which is all true, and yet Mr. Atkins doth appear to be a very innocent man in this matter."

It was simply a case of misplaced zeal and mistaken identity. No one was to blame for Sam Atkins's sixteen weeks in prison, his chains, and his agony of mind and body–no one but that universal scapegoat, "the people."

The trial was over. While Sam stood at the bar with Captain Richardson at his side, the jury conferred without leaving the box. On the first charge, as principal in the murder, the verdict, according to instructions, was "Not Guilty."

"Down on your knees," whispered Captain Richardson. Sam Atkins fell to his knees and cried, according to form, "God bless the King and this honorable court." On the second charge, as an accessory to murder, the verdict was again "Not guilty." Once more Sam Atkins fell to his knees and cried fervently, "God bless the King and this honorable court!"

"Mr. Atkins," said Scroggs, "I should have been very glad that the rest, who have been condemned, had been as innocent as you are, and I do assure you I wish all man-kind had been innocent. For if any Protestant had been guilty of such a thing as this is, it would have grieved me to the very heart that any Protestant should do such things as those priests provoke their proselytes to do this day."

"My lord," said Captain Vittles, "here is his schoolmaster will give your lordship an account how he was bred and brought up, and what a good conditioned young man he was."

"Well, well, captain," said Scroggs with a crocodile smile, "go and drink a bottle with him."

There was no applause from the small crowd of disappointed spectators below the court. Sam turned from the bar to meet the smiles and embraces of his friends, but he was not yet free. He had to go back to Newgate, settle his bills, and pay his discharge fee to Captain Richardson. He was still in a daze.

In the interests of romance it would be pleasant to record that Sam Atkins's first action (after a bottle of wine and a good dinner) was to meet Sally Williams and renew his affair with her. Perhaps he did—contrite vows made in the shadow of death rarely last—but unlike his illustrious master, Sam kept no diary.

Sam should have been happy. He was free, God be thanked!—and good Mr. Pepys, who knew how much he owed to his clerk's stubborn courage, forgave him his sins, took him back into favor, and set him to work anew. His friends welcomed him back, and there were still convivial evenings at the Blue Posts and the Rose in Covent Garden. But there was no hero's welcome for him, no testimonial dinners or other rewards. The pawn who had blocked Lord Shaftesbury's plans and unwittingly saved Secretary Pepys and the Duke of York was still only a pawn. Sam was wiser, perhaps, after his painful experience—certainly he was more mature—but he was many pounds out of pocket and his health was impaired.

Moreover, the injustice of the court's proceedings, which had kept him from proving his innocence to the world and destroying Charles Atkins, still rankled. (Sam was always at his best when he had an audience for oratory.) To the London rabble he was still an object of suspicion, in spite of his acquittal. As one newswriter said, after announcing the convictions of Green, Berry, and Hill, "Mr. Atkins was also tried for the same murder, but the evidence not being clear against him he was acquitted."

"Not being clear!" What a scurvy, grudging, invidious statement!

The King's chief witnesses—Oates, Bedloe, and Prance—had written and published their "True Narratives," exposing all the horrors of the Popish Plot and the murder of Sir Edmund Godfrey. Why shouldn't Sam Atkins write and publish his own true narrative and so justify himself to the world while exposing Charles Atkins as a liar and a poltroon?

Much of the material he would need was already at hand. We can be sure that energetic Mr. Pepys had secured copies of Charles Atkins's depositions, plus various sworn statements from others about the captain's infamous conduct. From "the gentleman employed by my Lord Chief Justice on those occasions" Sam secured a stenographic copy of his trial. From John Child, now freed from Newgate but living in abject poverty, came a sworn statement that the sailor had never seen Sam Atkins until both appeared before the Secret Committee, and that Charles Atkins's story was a lie from start to finish. From a King's Messenger, John Bradley, and from two reputable merchants, John Aldridge and William Bowtell, all of whom had had dealings with Charles and could quote his very words, Sam secured "narratives" showing how Charles had swaggered, boasted, cheated, and lied.

Thus equipped, and boiling with indignation, Sam set to work. We have the original draught of his "Short Narrative," lacking depositions and the witnesses' "naratives." Evidently written at white heat in long, involved, and sometimes confused sentences, the document summarizes and refutes all the charges made against the writer (with frequent appeals to God to bear witness that he is telling the truth), and sets forth at length the story of Charles Atkins's cowardly conduct as captain of the *Quaker.* Clearly Sam was as much concerned with revenge —no small pleasure—as with vindication. He concluded with a sweeping summary and an unprovable charge against Charles Atkins:

"I think the irreparable injury I have received from this cursed story and invention of Charles Atkins (to the like of which every man in England was in this case with equal probability as subject as I, and is at this day in any other [case], while there be such a villain living) is evidently manifest, as well as the necessitous condition of Charles Atkins to put him upon it, the reward and other great advantages expected from it, the improbability of my being concerned, in that I am of another profession in religion and was never under any sort of necessity to invite me, the impossibility of my saying the words to Charles Atkins proved from my not having seen him in such a time, from my never having seen or heard of Child, and from the credit I hope my solemn asserverations and protestations made formerly to Dr. Tillotson and others under the circumstances I was then and repeat now here may find with honest men. To all which only take this one word of truth which I can unanswerably prove if anyone doubt it. I have evidence that this Charles Atkins was bred at St. Omers or some other part of Flanders in the Catholic religion, professed it all his life, and is at this day a Papist if he be anything."

The "Short Narrative of Samuel Atkins, his Case" was never published, perhaps because Mr. Pepys, preferring to let lying dogs sleep, thought it unwise. Charles Atkins went his swaggering way unpunished. Now Lieutenant Atkins of Sir John Fenwick's Regiment of Foot, he was never court-martialled for his cowardice; as an army officer and a King's witness, he was safely out of Mr. Pepys's reach. After Sam's trial he drops out of sight. We do not know the date of his death, but it must have been before 1688. After his name in a list of Naval officers from 1660 to 1688 appears this note, "Turned out for submitting himself to be towed in by the Turks. Dead." Let that be his epitaph.

Through 1679 the Popish Plot terror raged on unchecked. On February 21, Hill and Green were hanged at Tyburn; Berry was reprieved until the twenty-eighth. In the election for members of the new House of Commons, the Opposition party swept the polls, and to avert civil war King Charles sent the Duke of York into exile on the continent. On March 6, Parliament convened, with a still greater republican majority in the House of Commons. On April 20, King Charles, discouraged by the failure of reason and moderation, dismissed his ministers and turned the government over to the Opposition, with Lord Shaftesbury as President of an enlarged Privy Council. (In fact, affairs were directed from the King's Head tavern in Fleet Street, where the republican Green Ribbon Club had its headquarters.) A fresh Admiralty Commission of seven men—all but one republicans—took over at Derby House. On May 8, Thomas Pickering, who had been convicted of high treason on December 17, 1678, was finally hanged, drawn, and quartered at Tyburn.

Lord Shaftesbury had not finished with Mr. Pepys. For some time the Secretary, badgered by his new Admiralty Board and by a Parliamentary Committee to enquire into miscarriages in the navy, wanted to resign. He did so on May 21, just one day before the rabid House of Commons committed him and a colleague, Commissioner Sir Anthony Dean, to the Tower. The Opposition grandees had paid a rascally informer who called himself Colonel John Scott to swear that Pepys and Dean had hired a privateer to prey on English shipping in the last Dutch war, and that both had sold naval secrets, including maps of English coasts and harbors, to the French. In addition, Mr. Pepys's former butler, John James (who had been dismissed when he was caught in bed with Pepys's housekeeper), was paid to swear that Pepys was a secret Catholic and that his musician, Morelli, was probably a Jesuit. Pepys was accused of felony, piracy, Popery, and treason.

While Pepys and Dean fretted in the Tower, and Sam Atkins labored on unhappily at Derby House under a new Secretary, Thomas Hayter, the republican politicians kept the fires of religious hatred flaming with new trials.

On June 13, Whitebred and Fenwick, who had been tried once before, and three new Jesuit victims, Gavan, Harcourt, and Turner, were tried at the Old Bailey and convicted. The next day Richard Langhorne, a Catholic barrister accused by Oates of raising a Papist army to invade England, was tried and, of course, convicted. On June 21 the five Jesuits were executed before an immense press of exultant Londoners. Langhorne was executed on July 14. Shaftesbury kept the London mobs happy with blood and carcasses.

From his cell in the Tower, Mr. Pepys launched a large-scale investigation of the lurid life of his accuser, "Colonel" John Scott. His agents soon discovered that Scott had an international reputation as bully, lecher, thief, liar, forger, bigamist, and swindler. On July 9, when the Attorney General, fearing what might come out about Scott if he appeared as a witness, failed to press charges, Pepys and Dean were admitted to bail in the amount of £ 30,000 each.

By now the Popish Plot terror had reached its high-water mark and was beginning to ebb. On July 18, when the Queen's physician, Sir George Wakeman, and three Benedictine brothers endured a tedious, nine-hour-long trial, all were acquitted, largely because Lord Chief Justice Scroggs, either suspecting that the tide had turned or fed to the teeth with Titus Oates, found fault with the Savior of the Nation and was almost impartial in his summing up to the jury.

Early in the summer of 1679, the new Admiralty Commission discharged Sam Atkins without reason and without a single complaint about his "want of faithfulness, diligence, or ability." Shortly thereafter, his constitution weakened by his months in Newgate, Sam fell sick of a virulent ague. Thanks to his physicians, whose treatment for a fever was regular and copious bleeding (plus occasional use of quinine—"the Jesuits' powder") Sam was out of action for the next thirteen months.

Tossing on his fevered bed, he missed all the excitement of the following autumn and winter: the great procession on November 17 when thousands of republicans—now called Whigs—carried a huge effigy of the Pope through the City streets and burned it at Temple Bar, with live cats in its belly to squall and scream in the flames; the furor in Parliament as the Whigs tried vainly to pass a bill excluding the Duke of York from the succession to the throne; the trial and conviction of six secular priests on January 17, 1680; and Shaftesbury's dramatic disclosure in March of a Popish Plot in Ireland. Thoughtful men despaired of the future for an England bogged down in bigotry and torn by fear and faction.

Even in the midst of his own troubles, Mr. Pepys found time and energy to procure a pension for Betty Martin, his former mistress and Consul Martin's widow. His efforts resulted (on July 22, 1680) in a Privy Seal warrant for £100 a year to "Elizabeth Martin, relict of Samuel Martin, Esq., deceased, late Consul at Algiers."

But Mr. Pepys could do little for poor John Child, who sent him a begging letter, complaining that because of Charles Atkins's false accusation Child had lost all his friends and had been reduced to great extremity and want. Knowing Mr. Pepys's charitable inclinations, we can be sure that he sent Child a sum of money from his own straitened purse.

On June 30, 1680, Mr. Pepys and Sir Anthony Dean were finally discharged without a trial. Like Sam Atkins they never had a chance to prove their innocence; however, after fourteen months of persecution and fear, they were free men again, God be thanked!

By the summer of 1680, Sam Atkins, although still very weak, had recovered enough to worry about his future. On the advice of friends he petitioned the King for the office of Purveyor of the Petty Emptions—a minor clerk charged with the duty of providing small items for the navy. When that effort failed, he petitioned the Lords Commissioners of the Admiralty for the post of Judge Advocate—the naval equivalent of an attorney general. With his knowledge of Latin and of navy regulations, plus his recent experience with civil law, he was well qualified for the job. (The post paid ten shillings a day, or £182 10s. per year, a comfortable sum in those days.) He was willing, he said, to take on the duties of Petty Emptions as well, thus saving the navy £130 a year. That petition failed also—to the Admiralty Lords, Sam was still "Mr. Pepys' clerk," sharing his former master's disgrace—and as the summer drew toward autumn, he faced a bleak and dreary winter. He was pale and emaciated, unemployed, and deeply in debt.

A good friend came to his rescue. Captain David Lloyd, appointed on October 20 to command the *Crowne,* a large frigate, was soon to sail for the Mediterranean and the never-ending war with Barbary pirates. He proposed that Sam go with him as a volunteer or "reformado," a gentleman who ranked as an officer, but without pay and with very few duties. Thus Sam could learn all about the ways of the navy at first hand, and, with luck, after a voyage or two, could be appointed a lieutenant. In addition, Will Hewer, now Treasurer of Tangier, promised to do Sam "some good office in the Treasury" at Tangier.

On November 4, Sam wrote to Mr. Pepys, then at Brampton, detailing his plans and begging for the loan of £20 to provide a bed, linen, clothes, and other necessities for the voyage and for his expenses to Portsmouth. "Your favor in which," Sam concluded, "will (I trust in God) be a means to put me in some condition ere long of overcoming the series of ill fortune I have been crushed with."

To save time, Mr. Pepys wrote directly to Will Hewer in London, enclosing a copy of the letter from Sam Atkins, "whose hard fortune," he wrote, "I do heartily bemoan and do think myself obliged to give my assistance and everything I can towards his relief." He asked Hewer to give Sam the £20 in his behalf, "for I say again his case deserves all manner of compassion and above all from me; for certainly no youth of his wit and straitness of fortune ever withstood such temptations to have been a villain as that poor creature has done, and I hope God will bless him accordingly." On December 18, 1680, as Sam Atkins was about to sail, Mr. Pepys wrote also to his old friend Henry Shere, the great engineer then at Tangier, recommending Sam and asking Shere to give him all the help and friendship he could. He made it clear that Sam was seeking experience at sea, "hoping, it may please God, that before his return hither his country may be as well amended in its capacity of encouraging him as he is improved for the serving it."

For the next four years Sam Atkin's life was bounded by Tangier and the Mediterranean Fleet. He could only hear from afar of the gradual breaking up of the Popish Plot terror after the trial and execution of the Catholic Viscount Stafford; the defeat of the Exclusion Bill in the House of Lords (largely by the eloquence of Lord Halifax, who was no longer a member of the opposition); and the dissolution of the Oxford Parliament on March 28, 1681. For the next four years King Charles reigned without a Parliament.

Now, with the aid of subsidies from France and a nationwide reaction in England, the King turned the tables on the Whigs. He brought York back from the continent and sent him to govern Scotland, dismissed the leading Whigs from his Household, the Privy Council, and the Admiralty Commission, and lodged some of them in the Tower. Shaftesbury, freed by a packed London grand jury from a charge of high treason, fled abroad; he died in Holland in January, 1683.

Whig informers were out of fashion. Mr. Pepys's ex-butler, John James, died in March, 1680, confessing all his lies. Captain Bedloe, formed a harder metal, died unrepentant in August of that year. In 1681, Colonel John Scott fled from England to avoid trial for murdering a coachman. By 1683, Oates and his fellows were discredited and starving. Two years later Oates was convicted of perjury. He was fined, pilloried, whipped at the cart's tail, and imprisoned, with the added proviso that he should be pilloried five times in every year. The wheel had come full circle.

But none of these affairs mattered much to Sam Atkins. At twenty-three he had moved into a new world of shipboard fare, sailors' lingo, storms, and battles. Escaping from the gray skies and chill of an English winter to the warmth of the sunny Mediterranean, Sam recovered his health quickly. He found life pleasant and exciting as the *Crowne* ploughed the waves in search of Algerine galleys.

Unfortunately, his hopes of preferment in the navy were dashed by the fact that Admiral Arthur Herbert, commander of the Mediterranean Fleet, was one of Mr. Pepys's bitterest enemies. Herbert, a vicious, drunken, whoring courtier, extended his ill will to Mr. Pepys's former clerk and refused him an officer's commission. (In Mr. Pepys's opinion, "Of all the worst men living, Herbert is the only man that I do not know to have any one virtue to compound for all his vices.")

On February 15, 1681, Sam found some consolation in the fact that, through Will Hewer's influence, he was commissioned as an ensign in the Tangier Regiment of Foot. Now at least he had some standing and a small but sure income. His tolerant superior officers permitted him to continue his voyages as a volunteer in the *Crowne* with Captain Lloyd and his lieutenant, Thomas Leighton. On August 15, 1681, in a letter to Mr. Pepys, Sam complained about the admiral's biased behavior and added, "The whole satisfaction and quiet I have is in being in this ship with Lloyd and Leighton, who are much the best men of this sort I ever met with." He was enthusiastic about Captain Lloyd, "the best governed, soberest, reasonable man my conversation ever fell with," and about the discipline of his ship, "nor ever was the King master of so well disciplined, civil, and sober ship as this we swim in."

Mr. Pepys answered this letter on September 5. The master advised his former clerk to avoid conflict with Admiral Herbert, to improve his "sea-skill" as much as he could, and to add French to his Latin. He reminded Sam that not only Mr. Hewer and he, but the King, the Duke, and the new Lords Commissioners of the Admiralty were well disposed toward him and would not forget his "sufferings and deservings." He concluded by recommending Sam to God's protection "in a virtuous pursuit of your better fortune." It was a kind, friendly letter; unfortunately it never reached Sam Atkins.

In his voyages with Captain Lloyd, Sam was several times under fire and behaved very well. On January 1, 1682, he enclosed with a letter to Mr. Pepys his account of a battle that resulted in the capture of an Algerine war ship, the *Red Lion*, with 175 men and 24 guns. Since its captors, the *Crowne* and the *Sapphire*, were large frigates with 42 guns each, it was hardly a great victory. The laconic, colorless quality of Sam's account suggests that it was a copy of the report he had written for Captain Lloyd to transmit to Admiral Herbert.

In spite of the admiral's enmity, Sam still hoped for a good post in the navy. When Captain Lloyd's lieutenant, Thomas Leighton, was given command of another Algerine prize, the *Two Lions,* the captain asked that Sam be appointed as his new lieutenant. The admiral flatly refused. On July 26, 1682, Sam wrote a long, angry letter to his old friend and former fellow clerk, John Walbanke, complaining about the admiral's conduct. Herbert had broken his promises, had ignored a letter from the Admiralty Lords urging Sam's preferment, and had appointed a man "under far less recommendations" than he. Insultingly the admiral had offered Sam a post in the undesirable *James* galley. Sam had refused with what dignity and moderation he could muster. In his desperation, Sam begged Walbanke to get him an appointment as a Midshipman Extraordinary in Lloyd's ship. He was too old for an ordinary midshipman's berth.

In his last letter to Mr. Pepys from Tangier, dated March 8, 1683, Sam complained that since he left England he had received not one word from either Mr. Pepys or Will Hewer, although he had written several letters to each. His mood was somber. Peace with Algiers had been negotiated in April, 1682, and now that the dangerous sea action was over, he was limited to garrison duty at Tangier and could no longer hope for a post in the navy. After nearly three years abroad, longing for home, he was still in debt and was only an ensign in the Tangier Regiment of Foot, now under the command of the new governor, Colonel Percy Kirke, a brutal, profane, drunken libertine. There seemed to be no future for Sam on land or at sea.

A few months later the tide of his fortune turned. King Charles, in sore financial straits, decided to abandon costly Tangier, evacuate the garrison and all European residents, and destroy Shere's great breakwater, "the Mole." To do the work, he sent a fleet commanded by George Legge, Lord Dartmouth, with the titles of Captain-General of the Forces in Africa and Governor of Tangier. With Dartmouth in his flagship, the *Grafton*, went Mr. Pepys as his secretary and chief adviser, Will Hewer to disburse cash, Henry Shere to destroy his own work, and Dr. Thomas Ken to light the way to Heaven. The fleet reached Tangier on September 14, 1683.

Mr. Pepys was shocked at what he found in Tangier— "nothing," he said, "but vice in the whole place of all sorts, for swearing, cursing, drinking, and whoring." Governor Kirke was a notable tippler, who introduced every remark with "God damn me." He had a harem of whores, and when he was with them, his wife, Lady Mary, would disport herself with one of her gallants. With such examples it is no wonder that officers drank, swore, and kept mistresses, and that common soldiers and sailors frequented the brothels of Tangier when they were sober enough to navigate.

Mr. Pepys learned also that the outpost had "plainly been a place to find only pretense for the employment of our ships upon their own business and the governors', to Cadiz and up and down, to the debauching of all our commanders and others, and particularly my Atkins, I hearing, by themselves and others every day, fresh instances of their debauchery." The "debauchery" consisted chiefly in making "good voyages," carrying goods and bullion for the profit of the officers. No doubt Sam Atkins had had a modest share in Captain Lloyd's illicit profits.

In spite of Sam's lapses from virtue, Mr. Pepys befriended him and got him a double appointment: as Judge Advocate for the fleet and as joint secretary to Lord Dartmouth. With his secretary's salary to eke out his ensign's pay, Sam was almost prosperous. Eventually the Treasury paid him £71 10s. for his work as Judge Advocate.

More good fortune was to come. On March 30, 1684, Dartmouth's fleet, with Colonel Kirke's regiment aboard, arrived in England. Two months later King Charles dismissed the incompetent Admiralty Commission, took the post of Lord High Admiral himself, and appointed Mr. Pepys Secretary for the Affairs of the Admiralty of England, at a salary of £2,000 a year—worth ten times that much today. Once again Pepys was master of England's far-flung navy. He brought Sam Atkins into his office and set about reforming and rebuilding the neglected navy, a herculean task but not beyond his powers.

Back in his proper environment, Sam Atkins's sturdy Puritan integrity became dominant again. For five years he had suffered humiliation and imprisonment, a trial for his life, unjust dismissal, prolonged sickness, battles, the spurns that patient merit took from the unworthy, and the temptations of Tangier. He had few illusions left.

Time had dulled his bitterness about his sixteen weeks in Newgate, and he rarely gave a thought to the now extinct Popish Plot. But in April, 1686, a remarkable event reminded him of the murder of Sir Edmund Godfrey. Miles Prance, unable longer to endure the prickings of his conscience, voluntarily admitted that he had lied, that everything he had said about the murder was false. On May 14 he pleaded guilty to an indictment for perjury; he was pilloried and whipped. Shocked by the news, Sam Atkins was confirmed in his belief that there was no faith in man. However, he still trusted in God—and Mr. Pepys.

Through the last year of King Charles's reign and the four troubled years of bigoted, priest-ridden King James II, Mr. Pepys and his favorite clerk labored together. Sam Atkins was Mr. Pepys's righthand man, and (after Will Hewer became a Special Commissioner of the Navy) he became Pepys's chief clerk and head of his office, now at York Buildings in the Strand, when the Secretary was absent. Sam's years of training and his experiences in the Mediterranean stood him in good stead.

In February, 1689, after King James had fled to France and the dust of the Glorious Revolution had settled, Mr. Pepys, too intimately associated with James II to be kept as Secretary under King William and Queen Mary, resigned his office and retired to private life. Sam Atkins continued his career as a public servant, but his long association with Mr. Pepys was never forgotten. In April, 1700, when the House of Lords appointed five men to serve on a commission for army debts, Narcissus Luttrell reported that one of the five was "Mr. Sam: Atkins, formerly clerk to Secretary Pepys." On February 8, 1702, Sam was appointed a Commissioner of the Navy, perhaps through Mr. Pepys's influence.

Naturally enough, after the great Secretary resigned, master and clerk saw less of each other, but they remained good friends and sometimes dined together. On May 26, 1703, when Mr. Pepys died, full of years and honor, Sam Atkins was one of those who received both rings and mourning attire, and attended his beloved master to the grave.

Some time before June 19, 1696, when Sam Atkins made his will, he took a wife. In his will, after thriftily enjoining his wife to spend no more than ten pounds on his funeral, he left all his "goods and chattels, real and personal, and credits and estate whatsoever" to his "loving wife, Mary Atkins." Sam died in August, 1706, at the age of forty-nine. His will (now at Somerset

House) was probated on September 8; there is no mention of children.

Although Samuel Atkins, Mr. Pepys's clerk, became a considerable gentleman, known for integrity and industry, he was never considered among the great of his generation. At least, unlike most men, he had one moment of greatness.

Appendixes

Appendixes

Letters, 1676-1683

The originals of the following letters written by Samuel
Atkins are preserved among the Rawlinson Manuscripts,
Bodleian Library, Oxford University. I have expanded
contractions and modernized spelling and punctuation.

I

To Mr. Pepys [April 26, 1677]

May it please your honor.

I most humbly ask your forgiveness for this presump-
tion and pray your leave only to offer this one thing
in my behalf, which is, if you please to give me your
remission for my past miscarriages and the honor of
serving you once more, upon my first ill comportment,
or being (upon any occasion) found a minute out of
your house without your leave, I willingly lay this at
your feet as my own act to banish me forever your
service, favor, or countenance. By which (the strictness
of my performance hereof easily appearing to your
honor) I humbly hope you will be convinced that I
cannot hereafter be guilty of any of the crimes I now lie
under the marks of your displeasure for.

I beg your honor, for God's sake, to harken to this
my humblest suit, in which I am the more earnest as
being fully confident the resolutions and vows I lie

under to God Almighty will enable me perfectly to keep up to this I now humbly offer, and by which I may get your honor's favor and good opinion and preserve myself from despair and ruin. Withdraw, sir, I pray, your displeasure, and let time satisfy you 'tis in my nature (with God's assistance) to do this, and that 'tis on no slender grounds or want of a full assurance of my being able to comply herewith, I dare hazard that whereon my future well being and all the good I expect in this world depends. I pray God incline your honor to a gracious consideration hereof.

Your honor's most penitent and
submissive applicant,
S: Atkins.

II

To Mr. Pepys at Brampton, Huntingdonshire,
November 4, 1680

Honored Sir:

Captain David Lloyd being this day appointed to the command of the *Crowne* lying at Portsmouth and designed for the convoy of the Fish Ships[1] to the Straits in company with Captain [Morgan] Kempthorne[2] in the *Kingfisher,* whereon they are to proceed about the 15th of this month, I have fully resolved (with submission to your good liking) to take my fortune with him therein, being thereto encouraged by Mr. Hewer's kindness in his promises of doing me some good office in the Treasury at Tangier, when that

---

1. Captain David Lloyd was appointed on October 20, and took command of the *Crowne* on November 4. The "Fish Ships" were on their way to the Grand Banks, off Newfoundland. The war ships would convoy them only as far as the Straits of Gibraltar.

2. Captain Morgan Kempthorne was given command of the *Kingfisher,* a 4th rate, on October 21, 1679. Killed in battle.

affair comes to be settled; besides the expectations from Captain Herbert[3] and Sir Palmes Fairborne,[4] if anything lie in their way to do me a good turn; to help me in which it is that, for saving all the time that may be, I have addressed this trouble to you (under an uncertainty of your returning hither) to pray your favor to write to Scotland for his Royal Highness's letters to both of them in my behalf, to the former mentioning particularly (if you think fit) the business of the Judge Advocate.

To which I have one other prayer to add, and I hope to give you no more trouble, which is that my stock of credit with my friends and relations being wasted in my maintenance these thirteen months of illness, and a provision of bed, linen, clothes, and other necessaries fit for the voyage being to be made very quickly to enable me to go, you will please to order me here such a sum as twenty pounds for my doing that, and to support my necessary expenses to Portsmouth and from thence onward in the voyage. Your favor in which will (I trust in God) be a means to put me in some condition ere long of overcoming the series of ill fortune I have been crushed with, and shall constantly be owned as an indelible obligation among the many others you have placed on me, that am with all duty and regard, sir,

> Your ever obliged and most faithful
> humble servant.
> Sam Atkins

If you please to write, your letter will find me, directed to be left at Derby House.

---

3. "Captain" Herbert was actually Admiral Arthur Herbert, Commander-in-Chief in the Straits.

4. Sir Palmes Fairborne had spent eighteen years in the army at Tangier. He was killed by a musket shot on October 24, 1680. Obviously the news of his death had not yet reached England.

III

To Mr. Pepys

At sea off the Southward
Cape,[5] August 15, 1681.

Honored Sir,

Since the trouble I gave you from Naples of what had happened worth your notice in my voyage so far downwind as that place, nothing has fallen out that would excuse my interrupting you with a letter till this time, that I think it becomes me to let you know we are in safety got this far with our convoys, whom having seen as far further in their way as the latitude of the Rock of Lisbon, we are directed to leave under the care of Captain Wrenn[6] in the *Nonesuch*, and to return with the *Kingfisher* (now under the command of young Captain Wheeler[7], to the prosecution of what orders we shall find from the Admiral[8] at Tangier, which we left three days since in good condition, under a perfect peace with the Moors and a good degree of plenty of all sorts of provisions.

In my attendance upon the Admiral I wanted the letter in my favor from Scotland, which I pray your favor to hasten to me, though I find the ill will he bears you (notwithstanding your fair correspondencies) reaches to me, who am glad to be thought considerable enough to suffer for your sake, and shall never court favor nor friendship from one that I know with so little reason treats you so ill at this distance. But this usage from him to you is no other than many other worthy gentlemen have the like reason to

5. The Southward Cape was Cape St. Vincent, Portugal.

6. Captain Ralph Wrenn was appointed to command the *Nonesuch* on August 9, 1681.

7. Captain Francis Wheeler was appointed to command the *Kingfisher* on August 7, 1681, after Kempthorne's death.

8. Admiral Arthur Herbert, later Earl of Torrington.

complain of, particularly the late governor, Colonel Sack-vile,[9] Mr. Shere,[10] his quondam amigo, Captain Russell,[11] and, save a favorite or two, the whole fleet and garrison. The former is divided into two implacable factions, and the differences between them irreconcilable; his great jealousy and the attention he gives to stories from rascals employed to bring them make his carriage very intolerable, so as everybody grows weary, and the service in the mean time can boast of no advantage from it. This freedom in me I hope, sir, you will excuse, and take no notice of anything from me, who, if I have no favor from him, would yet be as quiet as I could while I continue under his command. His enmity to Mr. Shere was, I believe, the greatest reason that induced him to go with the hulk and stores to Gibraltar, though it must be allowed that place is much better for the service than I think Tangier can ever be made; but I have many reasons to doubt that consideration weighed now with him.

The whole satisfaction and quiet I have is in being in this ship with Lloyd and Leighton,[12] who are much the best men of this sort I ever met with, nor can I ever sufficiently own the former's friendship and kindness, of whom, without doing any sort of injury to truth, I may say he is the best governed, soberest, reasonable man my conversation ever fell with, nor ever was the King master of so well disciplined, civil, and sober ship as this we swim in, of whom with great verity I can say now what before I could not believe could truly have been said of any ship, as to her government and disposal for the King's honor and

9. Colonel Edward Sackvile succeeded Fairborne as governor of Tangier; he returned to England c. May, 1681.

10. Edward Shere was the engineer who finished the great Mole at Tangier and later destroyed it.

11. Captain Edward Russell was brother-in-law to William Harboard, who had sought to replace Mr. Pepys as Secretary.

12. Thomas Leighton, lieutenant of the *Crowne*, was appointed captain of a prize, the *Two Lions*, on July 17, 1682.

advantage. Forgive, sir, this digression, and as the chief
thing I covet in this world continue me in your good favor
and protection as, honored sir,

> Your ever obedient, faithful and
> humble servant,
> Sam Atkins

IV

To Mr. Pepys

Alicante Road,[13] January 1, 1681/2

Honored Sir:

At the desire of Captain Lloyd I should have troubled
you with a letter by young Dennis from Cadiz upon
occasion of his going home, but my being out of the
way prevented my doing it then, and till this having
no opportunity, I think it may become less necessary
now to do it, Captain Lloyd's to his father being, I
suppose, communicated to you, wherein I am sure he
has dealt truly and plainly with him, and though it be
an unwelcome tale to a parent, yet it must be less
surprising to him that had found so little good effects
of the pains he took while he was under his own im-
mediate care. I assure you, sir, no entreaties, admo-
nitions, threats, or the severest punishments ever worked
upon him; every day made him worse, and his crimes
were grown such as might be original ill examples to
the oldest man in the ship, to all which was added his
natural aversion and awkwardness to his trade, his labors
wherein (had he been otherwise fit to be kept in a ship)
would never have made him a philo-nauticus.

All the other trouble I have to give you is to hand
the enclosed account of our success against the Algerines
for your perusal, and to pray your favor to hasten to me

---

13. A protected anchorage near Alicante, a city in southeast Spain.

the letter from Scotland in my behalf to the Admiral, that I may do all I can to improve the good fortune God Almighty has now twice blessed me with, to some advantage of getting my bread one way or t'other.

I pray your favor to give my humblest services to Mr. Hewer, and to accept the like with all duty to yourself, whose commands I pray may be given me, if my labor or study in my many vacant hours can serve to render you any little services in these parts, or from this trade, for I am with all possible respect and sense of gratitude, honored sir,

Your ever faithful and
most obedient servant,
Sam Atkins.

[Enclosure]

December 18th, 1681. An account of the taking of the *Red Lion* of Argier by the *Crowne* frigate, D:Lloyd, commander, in company with the *Sapphire*[14] and *Cala bash*,[15] fireship.

At ten o'clock on Sunday night, the 18th day of December, standing to the southward with our starboard tacks on board, we made five sail: four to windward and one right ahead, with their larboard tacks on board standing to the northward, having then a fresh gale at west-south-west. We gave notice to the *Sapphire*, who was astern, and got our ship ready with all diligence. The ship ahead weathered us about a quarter of a mile; the four others tacked and stood as we did, and we having made a clear ship went about, thinking to fetch the sternmost, which was the first we saw. The *Calabash* likewise tacked, but the *Sapphire* stretched further to the

14. The frigate *Sapphire* was commanded by Captain Anthony Hastings, appointed April 22, 1681.

15. The *Calabash*, a small prize commanded by Captain Peter Pickard (appointed December 20, 1680), was sold as useless in December, 1684.

southward and then tacked. Between eleven and twelve the stern ship weathered us about three ships length; in passing we hailed him but had no answer. We got into his wake and tacked and stood after him; the like did the *Calabash* and at the same time the wind veered to the west. The *Sapphire* being about a mile ahead of us and standing to the northward, tacked and stood after the chase as we did. We run from the *Calabash* and by the *Sapphire* a great pace and fetched again on the chase; the ships to windward still kept their wind. Between twelve and one the chase paid away large, but we kept our course till we had the length of him, and the *Sapphire,* being fallen on our larboard quarter, paid with him. He therefore put right afore it and we and the *Sapphire* after him, she keeping him on her starboard and we on our larboard bow, and fetched faster on him, which he perceiving brought to and got his larboard tacks on board and stood close hauled to the northward, then put a light abroad which was answered by the ships astern with two lights and firing of three guns, distinctly one from t'other. His standing to the northward brought the *Sapphire* ahead of us, but we run under his lee and by two o'clock had half a mile ahead of her, and by our standing to the northward gave opportunity to the *Calabash* to join with us. At two o'clock the wind was very much dullard, which helped the chase to keep her own, nor was there any sensible difference then to be perceived between the chasers.

By three this morning we got near him and hailed him, which he answered in English by asking whence we were, and being told, we could get no further answer. We sounded our trumpet and fired a gun to make him stay, and the *Calabash* being got a-breast of us and somewhat to windward of him, fired guns, but the chase being in our wind we could not get further than just under his quarter. At four o'clock we rung our bell, and the like did the *Calabash* (the Turks never carrying or using any), upon which he quickly fired his stern chase at us, and we plied our fore chase, being much afraid of a calm which might give him opportunity to get from us with his oars. The *Calabash* also plied his guns, and the *Sapphire* did the like, being then about two cables length astern of us upon our weather quarter. At daybreak we put abroad our English and he his Turk's colors, being then shot a cables length ahead of us, but his sails and rigging being very much galled with our great and small shot gave him very little hopes of escaping. He therefore at nine o'clock got out his boat and rowed towards the ships to windward about two leagues, who shamefully kept hovering there without attempting to give the least relief to their companion or hopes to us of having a fling at them, which we greatly desired.

We got our boat out, and Mr, Leighton, Mr. Bulkeley, Mr. Elliott[16] and myself went in her, but the *Sapphire* being astern of us had the advantage of having his boat nearer to the enemy's, and the gale also freshening we were called and came back. The Turks to windward went about and stood away with all the sail they could, but seeing the boats, braced to, which made Captain Lloyd call to the *Sapphire* to go about and look after the boats, which he did. Between ten and eleven we got up to the prize. The *Calabash* attempted to lay him on board on the larboard bow but, he putting his helm a-weather, missed and shot ahead. At the same time we laid him on board with our bowsprit over his quarter abaft his mizzenmast, but our sprit sail not being handed, lest he should get away from us by our shortening sail, blinded us that our men who were ready upon the bowsprit-end could not enter, and he wearing caused our bowsprit to sweep away his staff and ensign, and we at that time poured our broadside and small shot into him, and he immediately

16. Probably Bulkeley and Elliott were midshipmen or reformadoes. James Elliott was appointed a lieutenant of the *Crowne* on July 17, 1682, and Thomas Bulkeley a lieutenant of the same ship on August 1, 1682.

called for quarter. The *Calabash* then backed astern and dropped in twelve men. We hauled up our sails and brought to and sent our boat with the lieutenant, the other gentlemen and myself, and took possession of her. In the meantime the rest of the Turks made what sail they could away, and the *Sapphire* took up her boat, who, after some dispute, had taken the Turk's boat with the captain and two lieutenants in her.

The prize is called the *Red Lion* of Argier, manned with 150 men, Moors and Turks, and 25 Christians (six wherof are English) and mounted with 24 guns. Great part of the Moors were killed or wounded, and the ship much torn in her sails and rigging. She left Argier but the Friday night past in company with four sail more and a settee,[17] one of which lost company. The other three were called the *Media-Morte*, a ship never before at sea, mounted with 40 guns and 38 pattereroes,[18] with above 500 men; the *Great Pearl* of 38 guns, 30 pattereroes and 400 men; the *Sampson* with 28 guns, 8 pattereroes and 100 men—all very clean ships, notwithstanding which and that we had been just seven weeks off of ground, we out-sailed them and took this by down-right running. The *Sapphire* gave chase to the ships to windward, but the night growing on, and they being, I believe, near three leagues in the wind's eye, she found it to no purpose and so gave it over.

17. A settee was a small single-decked ship with two masts and lateen sails.

18. Pattereroes, or perriers, were small, breach-loading guns.

V

To John Walbanke.[19]

Tangier, 26th July, 1682.

Dear Jack,

Notwithstanding what I wrote you by Captain Russell in the *Newcastle* of the hope I had then upon his and my other friends' intercession with the Admiral to be lieutenant to Lloyd, grounded upon his promises made to them and me, he has since the departure of Captain Russell refused the doing me that favor and put in another man as equal stranger to him as myself, and under far less recommendation than I was. The Governor here,[20] Aylmer,[21]Lloyd, and Russell before he went made as much intercession with him as would have made almost an admiral; nothing will do, he utterly refuses it, and would indeed have put me into the *James* galley, but that with the advice of my friends, after he having declared himself my enemy and done what he did, I refused with great modesty, resolving never to receive any favor from anybody with such prejudice to me as that must cause; he having declared that I nor anybody that ever had relation to Pepys could be his friend, although at the same time he has confessed he had inclinations to think well of me, but thought I must be corrupted as to his interest. I wrote to him and got no reply and delivered him a letter wherein I desired that he would not persist to do me injury if he designed me no good, for I was a young fellow depending upon my fair character in the world for my future fortune, and since he nor any man could deservedly say ill of me,

19. John Walbanke, long an Admiralty clerk, died in December, 1686.

20. The governor of Tangier was Colonel Percy Kirke, who succeeded Colonel Edward Sackvile.

21. Captain Matthew Aylmer was appointed on January 10, 1682, to command a prize, the *Tiger*.

I desired he would not make my fortune desperate, especially since his ill opinion of me proceeded from a reason I could not possibly help, which was my having had relation to Mr. Pepys, to whom he is an implacable enemy. Upon this letter he gave his word of honor to the Governor never to do me any ill office, though he could not be brought to do me good, with which very well satisfied I parted with him with a resolution never to receive or desire any favor from him, and I hope you nor any of my friends will think I stomach it too much, after the unkind and ungentlemanlike usage he has given me privately to my friends, but so as I could not take hold of it to justify myself, and though I had taken this, I was abused, he never would do me further kindness, and did this not for my sake but to be rid of the importunity of my friends that appeared so warmly to him for me. We cannot guess at any other reason he has to be so much my enemy, having always had good characters of me from all that knew me, but we are apt to think he would have Lloyd and I parted, who he thinks, perhaps, are too great friends, and that I may have advised him to do some things he has not liked. Whatever it be, I refused at first ever to leave him, nor will I till the fatal stroke part us, and had not stirred about being lieutenant had not he promised I should be so with Lloyd. I am thus tedious with you in this story because he has, I believe, wrote to the Commissioners to tell them that, in answer to their letter which was twelve months since, he would now have preferred me, and I refused it; so that you may have it in your power to do me right when it shall come to the Board and especially to Mr. [Edward] Hales [and] Sir Humphrey [Winch], and if they have it so represented as to think I have not done ill, I have no cause to repent; for indeed I would not, especially since the action is over and preferment so slow, be thought to have given over my pretentions to business by embracing a new trade at this time of day, but only by my being in this to have made myself fitter for the other, which I am sure I have done ninety in the hundred, and

I would not be without the experience I have to improve myself in business for twice as much hazard, labor, and pains as I have been at for this.

Pray, let Mr. Pepys know the whole affair, for I am loath to write myself, since I fear those I have already wrote have not been received as I hoped, having not ever since I left England seen a syllable from him or Mr. Hewer, to my great trouble and affliction. Pray you, consider my misery and relieve me as it falls in your power; especially let me know my business of the ship's done, that my debts be paid, and I in a condition to come and look after somewhat for myself, to which by Aylmer I have great encouragement from the Duke to believe he will do all he can when I come. I should think 'twould not be hard for you to get an order for my being borne with Lloyd as a Midshipman Extra, since the fight with the Turks in the *Kingfisher*. It would put a little money in my pocket at my return, and that, with my pay in the garrison and my debts paid, I might happily pass a little time with you till I could amend my fortune, which God send. Excuse this scribble, which I do in haste and the ships under sail, being unwilling to omit any occasion to let you know how affairs go here, and pray let me hear by the post to Cadiz from you, as the only comfort I meet here. The whole fleet are here, expecting the Admiral's orders, which nobody guesses at, but 'tis thought we shall all be going, which for Lloyd's sake with my soul I wish. My services to your lady and all my friends.

> Your most humble, affectionate
> and hearty friend,
> Sam: Atkins.

Don't expose this scribble, for I bear it here without making noise, especially at this time.

VI

To Mr. Pepys

Tangier, 8th March, 1682/3.

Sir,

Midst many difficulties and misfortunes I have met since I came abroad, that which has given me most sensible affliction is that I have not received one line from yourself or Mr. Hewer in answer to the two or three I took the liberty to trouble you with, and several to Mr. Hewer; of late indeed I have forborne any to either, not having had anything extraordinary to justify the trouble, and from (I hope) a false suspicion I had, grounded upon having no returns, that my former gave you some offense. The business of the lieutenancy and my difference with the Admiral I prayed Mr. Walbanke to communicate to you, and so shall not trouble you here about it, more than assuring you if I did it amiss, it was by the advice of my friends and intended otherwise; the manner of it, and many circumstances which I could not so well commit to paper, I prayed Captain Leighton, who was a witness here of them, to impart to you, and I believe he has by them convinced you I was not much in the wrong, though I confess from what has since happened, and from longer and better consideration, I have repented what, with the greatest provocation from the Admiral both with respect to yourself and me, I did. I am past all hopes of ever having any kindness from him, and have it only left to wish it may not be long in his power, especially in these parts, to do me any. In my governance in that and other matters your wise advice would be very welcome to me, and I hope I may not in vain expect, since I am ever resolved to follow it, and in everything studiously approve myself, honored sir,

Your very faithful and
most obedient servant
Sam: Atkins.

The Documents in the Case

I

Manuscript sources in the Bodleian Library, Oxford University

1. Atkins's "Account of the Passages at my several Examinations before the Committees of Lords and Commons," Rawlinson MS A 181, ff. 11-25. For a printed version with several variants see *A Complete Collection of State Trials,* VI, cols. 1473-92.

2. Atkins's "A Short Narrative of Samuel Atkins his Case," Rawlinson MS A 173, ff. 113-32.

3. Atkins's letters, Rawlinson MS A 161, f. 188; A 183, ff. 142, 190, 192, 194; A 178, ff. 184, 186.

4. Martin's letters and depositions by officers of the *Quaker,* Rawlinson MS A 173, ff. 133-37.

5. Pepys's "An Account of Atkins' Birth, Education, and Profession as to Protestancy," Rawlinson MS A 181, ff. 1-2.

6. Pepys's "The Method of Sam Atkins' Defense," Rawlinson MS A 181, ff. 25-26.

7. Pepys's letters, Rawlinson MS A 194, f. 225; f. 234; f. 257.

II

Other Sources

Bryant, Arthur, *Samuel Pepys, The Years of Peril,* 1935; *Samuel Pepys, The Savior of the Navy,* 1938.

Burnet, Gilbert, *History of My Own Times,* ed. Osmund Airy, 1900.

Calendars of State Papers, Domestic Series.

Calendars of Treasure Books.

Calendar of Wills, Prerogative Court of Canterbury, 1948.

Carr, John Dickson, *The Murder of Sir Edmund Bury Godfrey,* 1935.

Clowes, Wm. Laird, *The Royal Navy,* 1898.

Complete Collection of State Trials, A, ed. Thomas B. Howell, 1810.

Debates of the House of Commons, ed. Anchitel Grey, 1763.

Descriptive Catalogue of the Naval Manuscripts in the Pepysian Library, A, ed. J. R. Tanner, 4 vols., 1909.

Haley, K.H.D., *The First Earl of Shaftesbury,* 1968.

Harrison, Walter, *History of London,* 1776.

Hiscock, W.G. *John Evelyn and his Family Circle,* 1955.

Historical Manuscripts Commission: *Eleventh Report, House of Lords MS; Fifth Report,* Appendix.

Hooper, W. Eden, *History of Newgate and the Old Bailey, 1935.*

Journals of the House of Lords, XIII, 1675-81.

Lane, Jane, *Titus Oates,* 1949.

Lang, Andrew, "The Mystery of Sir Edmund Bury Godfrey," in *The Valet's Tragedy,* 1903.

Letters of Samuel Pepys, The, ed. H. T. Heath, 1955.

Letters and the Second Diary of Samuel Pepys, ed. R.G. Howarth, 1933.

Luttrell, Narcissus, *A Brief Historical Relation of State Affairs,* 6 vols., 1857.

Middlesex County Records, IV, ed. J. C. Jeaffreson, 1892.

New Dictionary of the Canting Crew, 1690.

"Newdigate Newsletters," Folger Shakespeare Library.

North, Roger, *Examen,* 1740.

Oates, Titus, *A Narrative of the Horrid Plot and Conspiracy of the Popish Party,* etc., 1679.

Ogg, David, *England in the Reign of Charles II,* 2 vols., 1934.

Pepys, Samuel, *Diary,* ed. H. B. Wheatley, 1893.

Playfair, R.L., *The Scourge of Christendom,* 1884.

Pollock, John, *The Popish Plot,* 1903.

Prance, Miles, *A True Narrative and Discovery of . . . the Horrid Popish Plot,* 1679.

Routh, M.A., *Tangier, 1661-84,* 1912.

Tangier Papers of Samuel Pepys, The, ed. Edwin Chappell, 1935.

Tanner, J.R. "Pepys and the Popish Plot," *English Historical Review,* 1892; *Mr. Pepys, An Introduction to the Diary,* 1925.

Wilson, J. H., "Samuel Pepys and Samuel Martin," *Notes and Queries,* February, 1960; *The Private Life of Mr. Pepys,* 1959.

Index

Index

Aldridge, John, 112

Alloway, Edward, 5

Atkins, Captain Charles; encounter with Algerines, 3; stays at Tangier, 10; arrested and bailed, 11; haunts Derby House, 12; becomes an informer, 26; confronts Sam Atkins, 34, 39; visits Sam in Newgate, 54, 64; commissioned a lieutenant, 92; testifies against Sam, 101; his death, 113

Atkins, Hannah, 13

Atkins, Sir Jonathan, 11, 12

Atkins, Samuel (the elder), 13

Atkins, Samuel, 6, 8, 13; his character, 14, 15, 25; examined by Secret Committee, 33; committed to Newgate, 41; before the lords again, 48; examined by a committee of Commons, 65; remembers his alibi, 67; indicted for murder, 78; his trial, 96; acquitted, 109; his "Short Narrative," 112; discharged and ill, 113; goes to sea, 118; at the Admiralty, 122; chief clerk, 123; dies, 123

Atkins, Susannah, 13, 54, 75

Aylmer, Captain Matthew, 137, 139

Bagwell, Mrs., 73

Bedloe, Captain William, 56; before the House of Lords, 57; confronts Sam Atkins, 59; a witness against Coleman, 81; accuses Prance, 87; at Atkins's trial, 103; his death, 118

Bellasis, John, Baron Belasyse of Worlaby, 56

Bennet, Thomas, 82

Berry, Henry, 87, 88, 94, 97, 99, 113

Beverly, Lieutenant John, 36

Birch, Colonel John, 65, 82

Bowman, Jethry, 5

Bowtell, William, 112

Bradley, John, 112

Bromwell, William, a baker, 64

Buckingham, George Villiers, Duke of, 32, 38, 59, 60, 61

Bulkeley, Thomas, 135

Bulstrode, Mrs., 68, 72, 75, 100

Burnet, Dr. Gilbert, 79

Carlisle, Charles Howard, Earl of, 13

Catherine, Queen, 7, 91

Charles II, King, 7, 20, 21, 23, 43, 57; dissolves the Long Parliament, 93; exiles the Duke of York, 114; abandons Tangier, 121

Child, John, 18, 26, 27, 34, 41, 112, 116

Child, Josiah, 34

Clange, John, 5

Coleman, Edward, 21, 80

Coniers, Father, 20

Coventry, Henry, 30, 31

Danby, Thomas Osborne, Earl of, 91

Dartmouth, George Legge, Baron, 121

Dean, Sir Anthony, 114, 116

Dickson, Richard, 75, 84

Dixworth, Captain, 3

Dolben, Justice Sir William, 98, 106

Dugdale, Stephen, 91

Elliott, James, 135
Essex, Arthur Capel, Earl of, 33, 34, 38
Evelyn, John, 8

Fairborne, Sir Palmes, 129
Fenwick, Father John, 85, 115
Francis, Robert, 5
French, William, 75, 84

Gavan, Father, 115
Gerard, Sir Gilbert, 65
Godfrey, Sir Edmund Bury, 22, 25, 28,
    et passim
Godfrey, Michael, 84
Green, Robert, 87, 88, 94, 97, 99, 113
Gregory, William, 65
Grove, John, 20, 85, 93
Gwyn, Nell, 13

Hales, Sir Edward, 138
Halifax, George Savile, Earl of, 33, 48,
    118
Harbord, William, 80
Harcourt, Father, 115
Hayes, John, 75, 77
Hayter, Thomas, 114
Herbert, Admiral Arthur, 119, 120,
    129, 130, 137
Hewer, William, 8, 14, 59, 100, 117,
    120, 121, 123
Hill, Lawrence, 87, 88, 94, 97, 99, 113
Homewood, Edward, 14, 38
Howard, Sir Philip, 13, 28, 29, 33, 40,
    52, 55, 58, 64

Howard, "Northern Tom," 13
Howe, John, 12
Hurst, Captain Henry, 18, 19, 36

Ireland, Father William, 85, 93

Jackson, Paulina, 83
James, John, 114, 118
Jeffreys, Sir George, 100
Jones, Attorney General Sir William,
    84, 98, 100, 102, 108
Joynes, William, 11

Kempthorne, Captain Morgan, 128
Ken, Dr. Thomas, 121
Ketch, Jack, 47, 70, 71, 89, 97, 99
Kirke, Lady Mary, 121
Kirke, Percy, 121, 137

Lane, Doll, 74
Langhorne, Richard, 115
Lawrence, a clerk, 8, 69
Leighton, Lieutenant Thomas, 119,
    120, 131, 135, 140
Lewis, a clerk, 8
Lion, a warder, 48, 74
Lloyd, Captain David, 68, 72, 98, 100,
    117, 119, 120, 122, 128, 131, 132, 137
Lloyd, Dr. William, 25, 89
London, Henry Compton, Bishop of,
    33, 52

Martin, Elizabeth, 9, 73, 116

Martin, Consul Samuel, 5, 6, 9, 17, 18
Middleton, Colonel Thomas, 14, 38
Monmouth, James, Duke of, 58, 83
Morelli, Caesare, 7, 82, 114

Narbrough, Sir John, 4
Naylor, Midshipman Giles, 5
North, Roger, 22, 25, 58

Oates, Titus, his history, 20; his dis-
   closures, 20; arrests Catholics, 21;
   "the Savior of the Nation," 22;
   witness against Coleman, 80; against
   priests, 85; convicted of perjury, 118
Orange, William, Prince of, 17, 58
Owens, Captain, 26, 27

Pembroke, Philip Herbert, Earl of, 22
Pepys, Elizabeth, 8
Pepys, Secretary Samuel, 6, 7, 9, 10;
   arrests Charles Atkins, 11; refuses
   him promotion, 12; at Newmarket,
   21; learns of Sam's arrest, 44; draws
   up an "Account", 46; collects
   evidence, 71; attacked in the House
   of Commons, 82; in prison, 114;
   discharged, 116; at Tangier, 121;
   Secretary of the Admiralty, 122;
   dies, 123
Pickering, Thomas, 20, 85, 93, 114
Pierce, Henry, 76
Player, Sir Thomas, 22
Powell, John, 92
Portsmouth, Louise Keroualle, Duchess
   of, 7, 13

Prance, Miles, 86; confesses murder,
   87; retracts and confesses again, 89,
   100; repents and confesses he lied,
   122

Richardson, Captain William, 41, 46,
   54, 61, 62, 70, 83, 89, 109
Richmond, Mary, Dowager Duchess
   of, 13
Roberts, a clerk, 8
Russell, Captain Edward, 131, 137

Sacheverel, William, 65, 66
Sackvile, Colonel Edward, 131
Scott, Colonel John, 114, 115, 118
Scroggs, Lord Chief Justice Sir Wil-
   liam, 80, 86, 95; presides at Sam
   Atkins's trial, 101
Shaftesbury, Anthony Ashley Cooper,
   Earl of, 23; heads Secret Committee,
   24; his old quarrel with Pepys, 29;
   examines Sam Atkins, 33; second
   examination, 48; third, 59; Presi-
   dent of the Privy Council, 114; flees
   abroad and dies, 118
Shere, Henry, 118, 131
Skinner, Daniel, 8
Skinner, Mary, 8, 74
Smith, Thomas, 31, 32
Smith, William, 89
Staley, William, 74, 79
Stafford, William Howard, Viscount,
   118
Stephenson, George, 75, 84
Stringer, Sir Thomas, 100

Tillotson, Dr. John, 91, 113
Tonge, Dr. Israel, 20
Tribbett, William, 84, 108
Turner, Father, 115

Vittles, Captain Richard, 67, 68, 69, 73, 75, 84, 100, 106, 110

Wakeman, Sir George, 91, 115
Walbanke, John, 8, 67, 69, 120, 140
Walters, John, 64
Walton, Thomas, 13, 104
Ward, Consul John, 6
Wheeler, Captain Francis, 130
Whitebread, Father Thomas, 85, 115
Wild, Justice Sir William, 99, 103, 108
Wildman, John, 59
Williams, Anne, 18, 68, 75, 107
Williams, Sarah, 18, 42, 68, 75, 76, 107, 111

Williamson, Sir Joseph, 26
Wilton, Thomas, 5
Winch, Sir Humphry, 138
Winchester, Charles Paulet, Marquis of, 33, 51
Winnington, Sir Francis, 100
Wrenn, Captain Ralph, 130

York, James Stuart, Duke of, 15, 17, 20, 114, 116, 123